Managing
Risk
in EXTREME
ENVIRONMENTS

Managing Risk
in EXTREME
ENVIRONMENTS

Front-line business
lessons for corporates
and financial institutions

Duncan Martin

KOGAN
PAGE

London and Philadelphia

Publisher's note

Every possible effort has been made to ensure that the information contained in this book is accurate at the time of going to press, and the publishers and author cannot accept responsibility for any errors or omissions, however caused. No responsibility for loss or damage occasioned to any person acting, or refraining from action, as a result of the material in this publication can be accepted by the editor, the publisher or the author.

First published in Great Britain and the United States in 2008 by Kogan Page Limited
Reprinted in 2008

120 Pentonville Road
London N1 9JN
United Kingdom
www.kogan-page.co.uk

525 South 4th Street, #241
Philadelphia PA 19147
USA

© Duncan Martin, 2008

ISBN 978 0 7494 4945 2

British Library Cataloguing-in-Publication Data

A CIP record for this book is available from the British Library.

Library of Congress Cataloging-in-Publication Data

Martin, Duncan.
   Managing risk in extreme environments : front-line business lessons for corporates and financial institutions / Duncan Martin.
       p. cm.
   Includes index.
   ISBN-13: 978-0-7494-4945-2
   1. Risk management. 2. Emergency management. I. Title.
   HD61.M28 2007
   658.15'5—dc22

                                                                2007037076

Typeset by JS Typesetting Ltd, Porthcawl, Mid Glamorgan
Printed and bound in Great Britain by MPG Books Ltd, Bodmin, Cornwall

Contents

Preface: One winter's day in Kabul

On 31 March 2004, insurgents killed four US security guards in Fallujah, Iraq. A crowd gathered and mutilated the bodies, then set them alight, dragged them round the city, and finally hung them from a bridge over the Euphrates. The incident invoked comparisons with the 'Black Hawk Down' incident in Mogadishu 1993, when a mob of Somalis killed and mutilated American soldiers and dragged them around the city, live on CNN.

A US security company had contracted the security guards to protect a convoy. The company's protection strategy was to use highly visible armoured vehicles and heavily armed personnel who responded aggressively to any perceived threat. This company believed in the power of deterrence: insurgents wouldn't attack because it was too dangerous.

The client firm that had in turn contracted the security company to protect its employees had for some time been concerned that deterrence was ineffective. Worse, it was concerned that making them such visible targets for the insurgents might even increase the danger to its employees. In particular, in the light of the increasing frequency of suicide bombings, it seemed unlikely that people who were prepared to kill themselves would be deterred by danger of death.

Shortly after the incident in Fallujah, the company changed its security contractor. The new contractor used beaten-up Iraqi vehicles, not brand-new white Land Cruisers. It dressed both guards and clients in Iraqi clothing, and its employees kept their weapons concealed unless they had to be used. Concealment was the centrepiece of the strategy: if the insurgents couldn't find you, they couldn't kill you.

RISK MANAGEMENT IN EXTREME ENVIRONMENTS

Regardless of the specific pros and cons of these two strategies – and there is a real debate, with real consequences – what struck me when I heard this story on a dreary Christmas day in Kabul in 2004 was that the core issue was risk management. However, this risk management was more vivid and more accessible than the highly abstract and mathematical version I practised day to day in my job in investment banking. For all of my 15 years in finance, first as a consultant and then a banker, it had always been difficult to explain what I did to non-specialists. In addition to the senior executives who were and are my clients, my parents, friends and in-laws all struggled to understand what I meant when I talked about risk and risk management.

Yet they understood what Sebastian Junger meant when he described *A Perfect Storm*, and every day they goggled at accounts of earthquakes, avian flu and terrorist attacks. Somehow people related to extreme events and extreme environments, so I thought perhaps there was an angle here. Perhaps I could use personal experiences in extreme environments to illustrate risk and risk management. I also thought there might be some lessons to be learnt professionally. Risk management in extreme environments might provide some insight on risk management in more mundane ones like banking. At the very least it would be fun to research, and I'd have a good answer ready if someone asked me to explain what I did at future Christmases in less exotic locations.

This book is the result. It is aimed at managers of risk, both those who call themselves risk managers and those who don't. The primary intention is to use life and death experiences in different extreme environments to illustrate and explain what risk management is, how it works and why it is important. I also intend to show that the study of risk management in extreme environments provides some lessons for risk management in mundane ones.

I hope to entertain while informing, and to give a window into extreme environments. To this end, I have tried to use the original words of my interviewees as far as possible, and to avoid academic prose, formulae and Greek symbols, and jargon. Please let me know whether it worked by email at duncan@lifeanddeathrisk.com.

Acknowledgements

I am deeply indebted to all those I interviewed in the course of the book, who so generously and patiently educated me on the specifics of their fields. In addition to those named at the beginning of each chapter in Part I, I'm grateful to Christopher Beese, Derek Bell, Charles Blackmore, Michael Bruce, Morrie Doughan, Russell Eggers, Gerry Elias, David Lambie, Ian McLaren, Josh Metlay, Trevor Morris, Simon Rowland, Beach Seakins, Colin Sharples, Mike Vivian, Jon Webb and several others who spoke to me but asked to remain anonymous.

I am almost as indebted to all those who helped me track down these interviewees and/or pointed me towards relevant secondary sources: Simon Boyden, Jo Carr, Rosy Cave, June Crown, Esi Dewitt, Ross Finlay, Susan Gibson, Edouard Girardet, David Hanke, David McCall, Kath McClellan, Iain Martin, Neville Martin, Sheenadh Martin, Santosh Menon, Sarah Milne, Tim Perry, Kevin Rosser, Dima Rozgonyuk, Ed Rylee, Helen Simpson, Penny Smith, Andrew Steel, Barbara Thomas and Eric Wolfe.

A particular thank you to Vasyl Rozgonyuk, his family, and his translator, Oleksiy Lutsyk. Without your help the meltdown chapter would have been impossible, and without that chapter the book might have remained unpublished.

Special thanks also to Brinley Bruton, Tim den Dekker, Jason Kofman and Jan Gooze-Zijl, who patiently read and commented on various versions of the manuscript.

I owe an intellectual debt to the writings of Naseem Taleb and Peter Bernstein, among others, and to my various bosses and mentors over the years, including Greg Fleming, Sunil Kappagoda, Bob Kopech, Peter Nakada, Konstantin von Schweinitz and Raj Singh. And finally thanks to all at Kogan Page, and to my agent Robert Dudley for believing in me and shepherding the book through the process from pitch to printed page.

Introduction

STUFF HAPPENS

What is risk? Risk is: stuff happens. Something unexpected, perhaps unexpectable, occurs. Thousands of miles from its source in southern China, SARS kills 38 people in Toronto; the nuclear reactor at Chernobyl is driven into a state that never even occurred to its designers, even as its operators disable critical safety features, and it explodes; events in the Middle East cause Britons to blow themselves up on the London Underground. The unexpected, the unthinkable, the impossible – they happen. This is risk. It is a fact of life, something we deal with every day, in every decision we take. We may take it out of choice, even in expectation of reward. Most often we take it because we have no choice.

This book is about risk management in extreme environments. What is risk management? Risk management is knowing your pain threshold, being prepared, and keeping your wits about you. Before an event, you need to know how much pain you can take. After it's happened, it's too late. Identify possible events, figure out how painful they will be, then make a plan to deal with them. Once you have the plan get the necessary resources, practise obsessively, and if the event happens, keep your head. Even if it's something you hadn't anticipated, if you have planned and practised, your odds of surviving are much better. Panic is usually worse than doing nothing.

What are extreme environments? Extreme environments are those where the stakes are life and death. You are an infectious disease consultant on an isolation ward in Toronto and your 'atypical pneumonia' patient isn't responding to antibiotics and is drowning in his own mucus. You are the off-duty deputy shift head when the reactor blows up, and you have to replace the on-duty shift head who's incoherent in hospital with radiation poisoning. You are the first responder on the platform after a bomb explodes on the London Tube and you have to decide who to save. An unconsidered decision in these circumstances might cost a life; a considered one might save it. In other words, managing risk in extreme environments is dealing with 'stuff' happening when life and death are at stake.

CORE CONCEPTS IN RISK

More formally, there are four core concepts in risk: frequency, severity, correlation and uncertainty.

An event is *frequent* if it occurs often. Most extreme events are mercifully infrequent. Historically, there is a severe earthquake (7 or greater on the Richter scale) about once every 25 years in California. Hence the frequency of big earthquakes in California is 1/25 or about 4 per cent each year.[1]

An event is *severe* if it causes a lot of damage. For example, according to the US Geological Survey (USGS), between 1900 and 2005 China experienced 13 severe earthquakes which in total killed an estimated 800,000 people; the 1920, 1927 and 1976 quakes each killed over 200,000 people. The average severity was 61,000 people killed.

Most people's perception of risk focuses on events that are low frequency and high severity, such as severe earthquakes, aircraft crashes and accidents at nuclear power plants. We feel that flying and nuclear power plants are risky since there is a small chance of a horrible accident. However, a fuller notion of risk includes two additional concepts: correlation and uncertainty.

Events are *correlated* if they tend to happen at the same time and place. For example, the flooding of New Orleans in 2005 was caused by a hurricane; the 1906 earthquake in San Francisco caused an enormous fire.

Estimates of frequency, severity and correlation are just that: estimates. They are usually based on past experience, and as investors know well, past performance offers no guarantees in the future. Similarly, the

---

[1] Note that frequency need not be measured over a time period. In many instances it is relevant to use other denominators. For example, in 30 years only two ejector seats failed on the UK Air Force planes, but then, the ejector seats were only rarely used. The relevant risk measure would have been how many times they would have failed had they been used. A survey revealed that several hundred ejector seats were faulty – accidents waiting to happen.

probabilities, severities and correlations of events in the future cannot be extrapolated with certainty from history: they are uncertain.

The rarer and more extreme the event, the greater the *uncertainty*. For example, according to the US National Oceanic and Atmospheric Administration, in the 105 years between 1900 and 2004 there were 25 severe (category 4 and 5) hurricanes in the United States. At the end of 2004, the frequency of a severe hurricane would have been estimated at 25/105, or about 24 per cent per year. However, there were four severe hurricanes in 2005 alone. Recalculating the frequency at the end of 2005, we end up with about 27 per cent per year (29/106). That's a large difference, and would have a material impact on preparations.[2]

Which estimate is correct, 24 per cent or 27 per cent? Neither, and both: uncertainty prohibits 'correctness'. Uncertainty is the essence of risk, and coping with it is the essence of risk management. Risk management in extreme environments is then predicting and managing the consequences of rare, severe and potentially correlated events under great uncertainty.

THINK, PLAN, DO

Risk management is a three-step process: Think, Plan, Do. The steps themselves are universal, the same everywhere, but exactly what they entail varies enormously.

Think

Thinking comes first. Before being able to manage risk, a risk manager must know how much risk is acceptable, and conversely at what stage to cut his or her losses. This appetite for risk is not self-evident. It is a philosophical choice, an issue of comfort with the frequency, severity and correlation of, and uncertainty around, potential events.

Different individuals, and different groups, have different preferences. Some people enjoy mountain climbing. They are comfortable with the knowledge that they are holding on to a small crack in a wet rock face with their fingertips and it's a long way down. Others prefer gardening, their feet firmly planted on the ground, their fingertips on their secateurs and not far from a cup of tea.

---

[2] With more data, uncertainty decreases. If we knew about 250 hurricanes over 1,050 years, the long-term average would be the same but the impact of the four hurricanes in 2005 would have been to change the odds from 250/1050 to 254/1051, an increase from 23.8 per cent to 24.2 per cent.

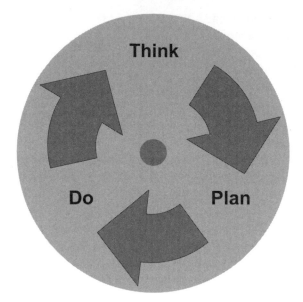

Figure 0.1   Think, Plan, Do

In the financial world, risk appetite simplifies to how much money an organization is prepared to lose before it cuts its losses. In life and death situations, it is the frequency with which a certain event results in death – the frequency and severity of fatal terrorist attacks in London, say. In some cases it is defined externally. For example, on oil rigs in the North Sea it is defined through legislation. Events that cause death more often than once in 10,000 years are not tolerable, and rig operators must mitigate the risk of any event with worse odds than this.

Plan

Planning is next. There are two parts: a strategic plan that matches resources and risks; and a tactical plan that assesses all the risks faced and details the response to each one.

The first part is the big picture. If, for example, you have decided that the frequency, severity and uncertainty of suicide bombings in London is too great, the big picture is that you need to change your life and move out of London, incurring whatever costs this requires. For organizations, the big picture has to dovetail with the organization's overall strategy. For example, although low-cost airlines need to be cheap, they cannot afford to cut corners on safety. Valujet discovered this when it was forced to ditch its brand following a catastrophic crash in 1996. Similarly, although the high command of the US Army Rangers recognizes that they operate in very dangerous environments – such as Mogadishu: see the preface – and hence will on occasion lose soldiers, they have adopted a policy of 'no man left behind'. This helps to ensure that in combat Rangers are less likely to surrender or retreat, perhaps as a result winning the day. Consequently airlines spend a lot on safety, and armies spend a lot on search and rescue capabilities.

The next stage is detailed planning. First, identify all the risks, all the things that might go wrong. Then assess and compare them to see which ones are the most likely and the most damaging. Finally, figure out what to do, who is going to do it, and how much it will cost.

California's state-wide disaster planning process is an excellent template for responding to extreme events, perhaps because of the high frequency of all manner of major incidents there – earthquakes, tsunamis, floods, wildfires, landslides, oil spills – you name it. State law specifies the extent of mutual aid between local communities, and requires each community to appoint a state-certified emergency manager. Each emergency manager creates a detailed disaster management and recovery plan for his or her local community, reflecting local issues and needs. These plans are audited by state inspectors and rolled up into a state-wide plan. The plan is input to the state budgeting process in order to obtain the necessary resources.

Critically, risk aversion does not necessarily make you safer. Many people or communities express a low risk appetite but baulk at the expense of reducing their risk to match their risk appetite. They don't put their money where their mouth is, and instead simply hope that the rare event doesn't happen. However, in the end, even rare events occur. The results of mismatching risk appetite and resources were devastatingly demonstrated recently as Hurricane Katrina drowned New Orleans.

Conversely, a large risk appetite is not the same thing as recklessness. A counterintuitive aspect of risk management in extreme environments is that although the individuals concerned are very comfortable with risk, they come across in conversation as somewhat risk averse. While they accept risk in the sense that 'everyone dies sometime', they work hard to eliminate or mitigate tangible risks as far as they can. They want to live – fully – for a long time. Anyone who does not manage risk very carefully in an extreme environment ends up dead fairly quickly, and is usually isolated within the risk group long before this happens. One former UK Special Forces officer relates the following episode:

> We were in the back of the Land Rover, expecting contact [a fight] any minute. Everyone was quiet, going through the plan in their heads,

controlling their fear – except for one bloke at the back, who was mouthing off. He hadn't been in a fight before and I guess this was his way of compensating. I decided that the first thing I would do when we got out of the Land Rover was hit him in the head with my rifle butt. He was too dangerous; I couldn't accept the risk that he posed to the operation.

Gareth Owen, the head of security at Save the Children, is pithier. 'Mavericks don't last', he says. It would seem that life imitates *Top Gun*.

Do

Doing is a combination of activities. Before an event, *doing* means being prepared. This consists of recruiting, training and rehearsing response teams; acquiring and positioning the appropriate equipment, communications systems and budget; and ensuring that both the public and the response teams know what to do and what not to do. After an event, *doing* means keeping your wits about you while implementing the tactical plan, managing the inevitable unexpected events that crop up, and to the extent possible, collecting data on the experience.

Once the epidemic has broken out or the earthquake has hit, the key is not to panic. Colin Sharples, a former Red Arrow acrobatic pilot and now the head of training and industry affairs at Britannia Airways, observes that instinctively 'your mind freezes for about 10 seconds in an emergency. Then it reboots'. Frozen individuals cannot help themselves or others. To counter this instinct, pilots are required go through a continuous and demanding training programme in flight simulators which 'covers all known scenarios, with the more critical ones, for example engine fires, covered every six months. Pilots who do not pass the test have to retrain'.

Most extreme environments have similar training programmes, albeit usually without the fancy hardware. As Davy Gunn of Glencoe Mountain Rescue puts it, 'Our training is to climb steep mountains in bad weather, because that's what we do [when we're called out]'. In addition to providing direct experience of extreme conditions, such training also increases skill levels to the point where difficult activities become routine, even reflexive. Together, the experience and the training allow team members to create some 'breathing space' with respect to the immediate danger. This breathing space ensures that team members can play their part and in addition preserve some spare mental capacity to cope with unexpected events.

The importance of this 'breathing space' reflex reflects a truth about many extreme situations: they don't usually start out that way. Rather, a 'chain of misfortune' builds up where one bad thing builds on another, and the situation turns from bad to critical to catastrophic. First, something bad happens. For example, a patient reports with novel symptoms and doesn't respond to treatment. Then the person dies, then one of his or her caregivers dies too. Then one of his or her relatives ends up in hospital with the same symptoms, and so on. A team with 'breathing space' can interrupt this chain by solving the problems at source as they arise, allowing them no time to compound. For example, a paranoid and suspicious infectious disease consultant (the best kind) might isolate the patient and implement strict patient/physician contact precautions before the infection is able to spread.

Closing the loop

When the *doing* is over and the situation has returned to normal, risk managers must close the loop and return to *thinking*. The group has to ask itself, 'So how did it go?' Using information collected centrally and participants' own experience, each part of the plan is evaluated against its original intention. This debrief can be formal or informal, depending on what works best. Sometimes it might even be public, such as the Cullen enquiry into the disastrous Piper Alpha North Sea oil platform fire in 1989, which cost 165 lives.

Where performance was bad, the group must question whether the cause was local – training, procedures and equipment – or strategic. Perhaps the situation was riskier than the organization wants to tolerate, or is able to afford. These conclusions feed into the next round of thinking and planning.

Thinking, planning and doing are usually group activities. Group structures vary from place to place, but most often there is a community at risk and an authority that manages that risk. In addition, there are usually various levels of authority, climbing a hierarchy. The upper levels of the hierarchy, such as national or provincial governments, dictate standards and maintain surplus people, equipment and money in reserve. The lower levels, such as cities or national parks, comply with the standards so they can call on these extra resources if they cannot cope by themselves. For example, city and state disaster management plans in the United States must comply with US Federal guidelines if the city or state wants the option of asking for Federal assistance in an emergency. Since each level maintains both plans and response capacity, thinking, planning and doing take place at all levels of the group. This creates major challenges in coordination, as we shall see later.

STRUCTURE OF THE BOOK

This book describes and analyses risk and risk management in nine extreme environments, and then links them together through common themes and the 'seven laws of extreme risk management'. Part I, Chapters 1 to 9, consists of nine case studies which analyse extreme environment risk management, from medicine to mining to mountain rescue. To help keep track of the various interviewees, each chapter has a list of those quoted at the front in the order in which they are quoted. These case studies illustrate and compare thinking, planning and doing in each environment, and draw parallels to risk management in more mundane environments such as banking.

Part II, from Chapter 10 onwards, describes the themes that cut across the case studies. Chapter 10 summarizes the case study findings. Chapter 11 offers some suggestions for risk management in the more mundane environments found in financial institutions and corporations. Chapter 12 closes the book, and boils down these findings to seven 'laws' about risk management from extreme environments that are universally applicable. At the end of the book there is a listing of useful resources for readers who want to follow up on any of the points raised.

The book can be read in any order. I recommend dipping into the case study that interests you most and taking it from there. Our story starts with the risk management of outbreaks of unknown infectious diseases.

Part I

Case Studies

1

Epidemic

Interviewees

Susan Coffin	Head of infectious disease control at the Children's Hospital of Pennsylvania in Philadelphia, USA
Alison McGeer	Consultant of infectious disease at Mount Sinai Hospital in Toronto, Canada
Geraldine Martell	Consultant in occupational health at Addenbrooke's Hospital in Cambridge, UK
Neil Rau	Infectious disease consultant at Credit Valley Hospital, Toronto, Canada
Sian Griffiths	Director of the Chinese University of Hong Kong School of Public Health, China
Sam Allen	Consultant in tropical medicine at the Westminster and Chelsea Hospital, London UK
Richard Fielding	Clinical psychologist at Hong Kong University, China
Penny Bevan	Head of emergency preparedness for the National Health Service, UK

Usually the work of an infectious disease physician is routine, not extreme. Rather it is 'gumshoe epidemiology', the bread-and-butter tasks of tracking down the cause of a patient's infection. 'Most of the time we have other problems under our nose', says Dr Susan Coffin, head of infectious disease control at the Children's Hospital of Pennsylvania in Philadelphia. Her day-to-day focus is to stay abreast of and implement the latest epidemiological research findings, for example improvements in treating newborns with a cardiac condition. This is the normal work pattern in her profession.

OUTBREAK

The routine work of epidemiologists is interrupted periodically and unpredictably by outbreaks of novel diseases. For example, in 2003 a previously unknown virus literally flew around the world. Apparently a severe, antibiotic-resistant form of pneumonia, it emerged in southern China in November 2002 and reached Hong Kong in January 2003. The virus was both highly contagious and highly debilitating. Healthcare workers (HCWs) were particularly vulnerable, accounting for a quarter of all cases. Hospitals became the principal channel for transmission; HCWs and patients alike stayed away. From Hong Kong it radiated out along global flight paths to 28 other countries, from Canada to Korea. Diagnosis was slow, as pneumonia is common in winter. Only in March 2003 did the World Health Organization (WHO) baptize the condition severe acute respiratory syndrome (SARS). By the end of the outbreak in July 2003 over 8,000 people had contracted the disease. Almost 800 died.

Dr Alison McGeer, consultant of infectious disease at Mount Sinai Hospital in Toronto, was on the front line of the fight against SARS in Canada:

> I knew when I took the first phone call that something big was happening. They told me that the gentleman [that we had been treating] had died and his family was ill. I knew it was a once-in-a-lifetime event. I can't say why, but I knew. I didn't know it was going to be so big, but I knew it was new. From the first case on March 13th until May 2nd it was nothing but the outbreak. Then there was a pause until the second phase broke on May 22nd and lasted until the end of June.

McGeer experienced the epidemic in two dramatically different ways:

> Academically it was tremendously exciting – this is what I do – it was an awesome and brilliant experience. With my infection control hat on, it was really, really difficult. It was my job to control infection and I signally failed to do that… it was really humbling. In the first two weeks I simply couldn't deliver what was necessary to protect people. There was no time to analyse what was I was feeling… I kept it compartmentalized so that I could keep functioning. There were endless things to do and they all had to be done yesterday. Everybody ran on adrenaline. One day I sat down at 6 am for my first conference call with Hong Kong, and at 5.30 pm I went downstairs to get breakfast.

In addition to her roles as researcher and practitioner, McGeer was also a patient. She contracted SARS in the middle of the outbreak – another HCW caught in the virus's path:

> I wasn't severely ill [although] for four days I wasn't doing much at all. For two weeks I suffered a significant reduction in function. I was in isolation for a month. The worse part was not being able to do what needed to be done… [but] there's a lot you can do by phone and internet [even from an isolation ward].

McGeer's experience illustrates how a previously unknown disease such as SARS can transform the infection control environment from routine to extreme. Physicians and other HCWs are comfortable not knowing what the precise disease is. Indeed, many appear to enjoy the thrill of the chase. However, they are not accustomed to confronting an unknown condition that threatens them directly. They are not used to being frightened. 'For most of my colleagues, the run-in with SARS was the first time they saw themselves as in danger. It never occurred to them that their work might put them at risk', says McGeer.

Patients are used to not knowing what is wrong with them. They go to doctors to get reassurance and a cure. They are not accustomed to their doctors being just as baffled. In these extreme conditions, there is a palpable sensation that the clock is ticking: as you search for a cure, your patients, your co-workers, your family and you personally are at risk. McGeer notes that 'at a personal level it was frightening – not what was happening to me, but the potential impact on family and friends'. In addition, in the face of the unknown, there is a nagging doubt. 'It was not clear for five or six weeks that we could control it.'

If you are fighting a fire, laying sandbags to control a flood or capping a blown-out oil well, what you are up against is tangible, elemental even: fire, water, earth. Not so for epidemics. The threat is invisible and spreads invisibly. In addition, successful management largely neutralizes a given, specific disease going forward. Natural selection and evolution continue, though, and new threats emerge over time. As a result, you never know which organism you will be up against next. This sense of the unknown is one reason why *thinking* about risk is more complex for epidemics than for most other extreme environments. As a result, we shall start our discussion with *doing*.

Faced with the sudden onset of an unknown, deadly and infectious disease, McGeer and her colleagues suspended normal activities. McGeer dedicated '100 per cent of my time for six months [exclusively to SARS] during the outbreak, then two whole years of [part-time] research. Basically it was a whole year of my professional life.'

The immediate challenge was twofold. First, alleviate patients' symptoms and stop them dying. Second, record and analyse the patients' data. What the medical staff learnt was that what killed people wasn't the virus itself, it was the 'cytokine storm' caused by the over-reaction of their own immune system.[1] As a result the treatment involved suppressing patients' own natural defences. Counterintuitively, they had to stop the body's immune system from responding in order to help the patient fight the disease. Eventually, the efforts of many teams of researchers around the world, coordinated by the WHO, led to the identification and characterization of the disease, and the development and adoption of common treatment and isolation protocols.

Alongside treatment and research, McGeer emphasizes three further imperatives for *doing*: containment, communication and detection.

Containment

Containment means preventing the infectious organism from jumping from human to human. For many routine conditions the most important part of containment is vaccination. McGeer notes that 'The biggest difference [in controlling an infectious disease] is from vaccinations.' Vaccines are a particularly attractive form of containment since they can be administered in advance. Indeed, smallpox vaccines are stockpiled in the United States to blunt a potential bioterrorist attack by 'ring vaccination' – the pre-emptive vaccination of all the contacts of an infected patient. However, like other medicines, vaccines require development, testing and manufacturing. These steps require a detailed understanding of the disease and some advance warning. For entirely new diseases they are not an option, and there are no guarantees. There is still no vaccine for SARS after three years of research. HIV (human immunodeficiency virus) has resisted attempts to create a vaccine for two decades.

In the absence of a vaccine or a cure, the only way to contain an outbreak is to completely physically isolate patients who may be infected. Isolated, they won't be able transmit the disease to anyone else. While there are many high-tech ways to do this – negative pressure wards, for example, from which the air is constantly extracted so that it can't

---

[1] Cytokine storms are not fully understood, but in essence the presence of a microbe stimulates the immune system. Cytokines are chemicals that transmit the request for immune response and activate the responding immune cells when they arrive. It appears that the signal sometimes gets jammed at 'on', causing perpetually escalating immune response. This build-up of immune cells inflames the lungs and blocks the air passages, causing breathing difficulties.

contaminate other wards, and the elaborate wearable plastic bags you see in the movies – most HCWs, like McGeer, emphasize 'the basics' such as handwashing. Rigorous handwashing prevents the disease stepping from patient to patient via HCWs' hands. For example, Dr Geraldine Martell, a consultant in occupational health at Addenbrooke's Hospital in Cambridge, UK, counsels that 'if you're faced with an outbreak of an unknown disease, you go back to basics: rigorously washing hands, wearing face masks, and cleaning and disposing of wastes. Do what you do anyway, and do it well.' Dr Wing Hong Seto of Queen Mary Hospital in Hong Kong advocated this approach early and aggressively. As a result Queen Mary Hospital suffered only two HCW SARS infections compared with at least 87 at the nearby Prince of Wales Hospital, according to the Hong Kong Government's SARS expert review.

The early identification and isolation of suspected patients is critical to containment. The means to do this are a major output from research efforts such as McGeer's. Researchers trawl through patient case notes to identify patterns of symptoms, transmission and treatment. As Dr Neil Rau, another infectious disease consultant in Toronto, puts it, 'The key question when faced with a new condition is how widespread is this already, now that we've discovered it? Usually if ye seek, ye shall find.'

Based on these findings, HCWs create a screening process to apply to incoming patients. Likely cases are isolated immediately; potential cases are logged and monitored. For example, the Ontario Centre for Disease Control (CDC) now has a one-page flow chart for SARS diagnosis and treatment based on four factors: coughing or shortness of breath, temperature above 38° Celsius, contact with a carrier or potential carrier, and a visit to a healthcare facility or country where an outbreak has occurred. This 'algorithm' is the basis for screening, admitting and treating patients as they arrive at the hospital. A patient with at least two of these risk factors will be admitted and isolated. Intermediate cases will be instructed to 'self-isolate', monitor their condition, and report back if not improving. Others will receive routine treatment. Importantly, both for research and for surveillance in those cases where transmission is possible, the local public health authorities are notified.

One of the tragedies of SARS was that Chinese HCWs had already gone through this process during the outbreak in Guangdong. For reasons that remain unclear – perhaps fear of inciting panic (see below), perhaps fear of punishment for having lost control of the situation – their knowledge and treatment protocols were never communicated, even within China. Consequently HCWs in Hong Kong and elsewhere had to reinvent these protocols at the height of the outbreak. (Fortunately the situation has since improved. According to Sian Griffiths, director of the Chinese University of Hong Kong School of Public Health and formerly the chair of the Hong Kong government's enquiry into the SARS outbreak, 'Cross-border cooperation across the border into China is much better now. Hong Kong is much more part of China now. They are much more open, although it is still hard to get statistics.')

During an outbreak, there is great pressure on the authorities to be seen to be doing something. Rau challenges the Ontario public health authorities' attempts to contain the SARS outbreak:

> In the incipient phases SARS was not recognized. It was a novel disease, with infection spread person to person and high mortality differentially affecting healthcare workers. Unabated it would have transferred between hospitals. The challenge was distinguishing SARS from other conditions. The reaction of the authorities in Ontario was to declare all hospitals on code orange – disaster management mode. All electives [operations to treat non-life-threatening conditions] were cancelled. Basically every patient was assumed to be a potential SARS patient and was screened for links to other SARS patients or hospitals where SARS had appeared.

This action strained the Ontario healthcare system severely. 'We should have had a tiered approach, and hospitals with no cases should have been allowed to function normally.' Rau is also critical of Ontario's early identification and isolation efforts. 'BC [British Columbia] managed to isolate the first person infected because the provincial CDC had put out a warning for a "mystery respiratory disease". Here we went from no reaction to overreaction.'

In addition to curtailing business-as-usual healthcare provision, containment raises civil liberties issues. Suspected patients have their right of free association suspended while they are isolated (assuming they had one in the first place). In most developed countries the laws are quite restrictive. In the United Kingdom for example, public health officials can apply for the examination, vaccination, quarantine or even detention of anyone suspected of infection with a 'notifiable' disease such as cholera or rabies under the Public Health (Control of Disease) Act 1984. In general, this is not an issue if a patient is clearly very sick. However, for less obvious conditions such as HIV it raises ethical questions: at what point does collective good outweigh individual freedom? This is part of the process of *thinking* about risk in this environment, of which more below.

Communication

The second element of *doing*, communication, walks a similarly fine line between reaction and overreaction. Patients require information to make decisions about their health. They need to know what the symptoms are, and what to do if they or those around them display them. They also require reassurance that the situation is under control, or else they may panic.

Unfortunately the situation is rarely binary – either under control or out of control – but somewhere in between. Gradual and subtle escalation in the threat level is difficult in public communications via mass media, especially if the latter are given to sensationalism (surely not?), and a population might tip into panic at some unexpected point. 'The biggest issue [in the management of serious infectious diseases] is press management' and not clinical management, observes Dr Sam Allen, a consultant in tropical medicine at the Westminster and Chelsea Hospital in London. A panicked, infectious population avoiding healthcare facilities, fleeing the epicentre of an epidemic and spreading it far and wide is probably the worst case scenario for infection control. It is this outcome that the Chinese authorities were presumably trying to avoid by withholding information.

Dr Richard Fielding, a clinical psychologist at Hong Kong University who studies public perceptions of risk from infectious disease, notes that 'The [Hong Kong] government was at pains to prevent panic. However, during SARS, it supplied reassurance beyond the point of credibility. They switched to damage control too late and the public lost confidence.' Hospital admissions in Hong Kong fell substantially as people figured out that hospitals were the most dangerous place to be. As a result, practitioners emphasize continuous communications with the public. For example, Sian Griffiths says:

> We should encourage healthy behaviours. [Since the SARS outbreak] the government has put a lot of effort into a public information campaign to reduce the chance of an epidemic by encouraging people to live more healthily – to exercise, get enough sleep, wear a mask if they're sick and not smoke. People have short memories, but their behaviour has changed.

Media handling plans are key components of communications plans. For example, the UK National Health Service's emergency planning guidelines have an entire chapter on media handling. The chapter states for example that 'media liaison and handling will be an integral part of planning a response to any major incident'. It also requires that 'Media protocols and Media Liaison Panels should be in place to ensure consistency of messages' and 'the identification... and training... of those officers with responsibility for media liaison'.

Communication to HCWs is also essential, McGeer notes:

> All healthcare workers need to know the risks to themselves and their
> patients, and what they can do. If you give healthcare workers the right
> information in the right way at the right time, they will make the right
> decisions. They want to make the patients better.

In contrast to the public, the risk is typically greater that HCWs will
underreact rather than overreact. McGeer continues: 'We [HCWs]
substantially ignore the risks. Even during the SARS outbreak in Toronto
healthcare workers were making risky decisions based on what they
thought they knew. We [doctors] live with decisions based on uncertainty
all the time. We're very comfortable with this.' Moreover 'there's an
element of wilfulness to it… we're not accustomed to doing what we're
told.' Training will help in the short term. McGeer suggests depressingly
that in the long term this behaviour may change as 'the pendulum swings
back towards infectious diseases' such as SARS and avian influenza in
developed countries. We shall come back to this resurgence of infectious
diseases later in the chapter.

Detection

Detection and surveillance together form the third leg of *doing*. During
an outbreak, case treatment protocols include notification of suspected
cases to the public health authorities. This allows the authorities to
conduct and coordinate case history analysis and to update protocols.
Outside an outbreak, a broad surveillance network allows early warning
of oncoming diseases – or at least of inexplicable health events that might
presage an emerging threat. For example, the Public Health Agency of
Canada runs the Global Public Health Intelligence Network (GPHIN).
GPHIN is a webcrawling programme which trawls internet news reports
in seven languages and flags potentially important items. The earlier
public health authorities become aware of a threat, and start to implement
containment and communication measures, the better. During SARS, the
WHO credited GPHIN with providing advance warning through its early
pick-up of news from Guangdong. Fielding emphasizes that 'if there is
an outbreak, we need to be on it asap, like a ton of bricks. The longer
the delay, the greater the probability that someone will get on a plane to
Jakarta, to Manila, to Los Angeles', and a local epidemic will become a
global pandemic.

More generally, in his view, 'the key issue in infectious disease control
is to maximize the distance between the agent [disease], the vector
[disease-carrying animal] and the host [us]'. He believes that 'our way of

life is intrinsically hazardous' because it fails to maximize this distance. He relates how 'Older people [in Hong Kong] say "When I was a kid in China, we had chickens dying all the time. What's the big deal?" Well, the deal is that when they were a kid there weren't 13 billion chickens in China.'

Griffiths takes this to the next logical step. For her, truly effective risk management must go further upstream into the environment in which the threat emerged – assuming that this upstream environment is known and understood. 'Managing the risk upstream is key... A lot of epidemic work is about containing something that hasn't happened yet. We have to shift our approach away from emergency response towards managing the food chain.' To combat diseases that originated on farms 'we have to change farming and food production practices such as immunization of poultry and how food is sold... for example live poultry sales in the wet markets... as well as focusing on [disease] identification at presentation, containment and epidemic management'.

Framing the challenge more broadly in this way highlights the size of the true underlying task: wherever you are in the world, if you want to manage the risk of SARS or avian flu properly, you need to change the behaviour of farmers and traders in China. That is, major risks will remain out of your control.

Many chickens cohabit with their owners, and often with their owners' pigs too. This happens all over the world, not just in China. As a result, in many poor rural areas, agents, vectors and hosts share a living room. This creates excellent conditions for different viruses to coinfect the same host animal, potentially swapping genes and becoming more exotic and more dangerous. In Fielding's view 'sooner or later something is going to slip under the radar screen and we won't be able to contain it... [just] like a Hollywood script'.

AN IMPLICIT RISK APPETITE

This breadth of scope is the other reason that *thinking* about risk is more complex for epidemics than for other extreme environments. Together, this breadth and the uncertainty we explored earlier mean that *thinking* about epidemic risk means thinking about the unpredictable emergence of diseases of unknown severity in uncontrollable environments all over the world.

At the time of writing, this is not a theoretical issue. At about the same time as the SARS virus emerged, a deadly new version of an existing avian influenza (flu) virus, H5N1, appeared in Southeast Asia. Killing both birds and humans, the virus spread west, apparently through migratory birds. By mid-2006 it had killed 132 people in 10 countries, and directly or through culls, over 100 million birds in 45 countries. While the human casualties have so far been modest, what is so frightening about H5N1 is that it has all the characteristics of a virus that could cause a pandemic – a global epidemic. In the 20th century there were three flu pandemics. Those in 1957 and 1968 were merely catastrophic, killing 1 million and 2 million people respectively. The pandemic of 1918 was truly apocalyptic, killing 20 million to 100 million people worldwide. If the current strain of H5N1 evolves the capacity for human-to-human transmission, it could cause similar havoc.

Risk managers can only manage what they control. They can create and maintain the infrastructure of containment, communication and surveillance in the areas that are under their control and for diseases that are known to them. Beyond that they manage each situation as it emerges, according to the evidence and resources available. Realistically, they cannot change the behaviour of millions of Chinese or Nigerian chicken farmers.

Penny Bevan, the head of emergency preparedness for the UK National Health Service, thinks that:

> The worst-case scenario, a flu pandemic in the UK similar to the 1918 pandemic would infect 24 to 30 million people and leave close to 1 million dead. We might consider draconian control measures such as closing schools and sealing borders.
>
> However, they would only be worth it if they provided enough breathing space to develop a vaccine. Creating a vaccine [for avian flu] would take four to six months with current techniques... [while these measures] would only buy two or three weeks. An evidence-based approach would indicate that they are not worthwhile.

In the middle of a flu pandemic:

> There would be a [ongoing] cost–benefit analysis. There are some obvious measures, such as cancelling all elective procedures and moving as many procedures as possible to outpatient or day surgery facilities. However, if the flu pandemic were serious, the benefits of these measures would be exhausted fairly early on. Then harder decisions would be required: what about cancer or heart disease patients where a deferral of six weeks might mean a death sentence?

This would likely be complicated by the fact that:

> Different parts of the United Kingdom would be hit by the pandemic at different times. Given the speed of transmission, it is possible that the south of England might be heavily affected, but the north of Scotland still relatively untouched. How would you explain to a patient that if only they'd lived somewhere else, their operation would still be available?

Should you save the life now, or ramp up for the lives to be saved when the disease goes national? Bevan is more worried by operational issues than clinical ones. 'The NHS is used to dealing with infection. We expect people to get infected and we are comfortable dealing with outbreaks.' In contrast, 'The biggest challenge [in a flu pandemic] would be business continuity.' If half the population has to take a week off work to recover from the flu, who's staffing the wards? Moreover, many supplies are delivered by truck. 'What happens if there are no truck drivers?' She does not have a detailed contingency plan for this scenario, since it is itself contingent on so many other things. In her emergency planning guidelines for NHS hospitals, Bevan advises that:

> It is the nature of major incidents that they are unpredictable and each will present a unique set of challenges. The task is not to anticipate them in detail. It is to have the expertise available and to have developed a set of core processes to handle the uncertainty and unpredictability of whatever happens.

Modelling epidemic spread

How does Bevan know how many infections and deaths would result in the worst-case scenario for H5N1? As in other extreme environments, there is a wide range of models available for experts to use.

The simplest models are known as Kermack-McKendrick SIR models, where S is the number of people in a population who are susceptible to a disease, I is the number infected and R is the number who have recovered. (The original SIR models assume a constant population and hence recovery rather than death. Subsequent extensions of these models can manage fatalities.) Transition between these states depends on the rates of transmission and recovery. Given a certain initial population split and these transition rates, the models predict how many people will be in each category (S, I or R) through the life of an outbreak. SIR models tend to show that highly infectious, high-mortality diseases such as Ebola spread rapidly (fast S to I) but burn themselves out rapidly too (fast I to R). Interestingly, in most cases the epidemic dies out for lack of infectives rather than susceptibles. The most dangerous diseases are those that infect slowly, kill slowly and offer no recovery, like HIV/AIDS.

An advantage of the SIR models in the pre-PC age was that they simplified to a set of equations that could be solved by hand. The latest generation of models, for example those referred to in the modelling of the effectiveness of 'ring vaccination' for smallpox following a terrorist incident, exploit cheap computer power to conduct large-scale simulations. They combine a detailed treatment of the specifics of the infectious disease – ease of transmission; natural and vaccine-acquired immunity and their efficacy; latent, symptomatic, infectious and recovery periods; morbidity and mortality; even parallel life cycles in other host organisms – with a detailed simulation of the chain of transmission through house-holds, schools and work places, and also of physician contact and treatment received. Each infected individual in a population is simulated for contacts, treatment and transmission in each period. Such simulations, if properly seeded, can provide critical input to public policy choices such as school closure, border sealing and prophylactic use of anti-viral drugs. However this is a big 'if': how do you model terrorist-spread smallpox when it has never happened?

At the back of many public health managers' minds surely looms the 'swine flu' fiasco in the United States in 1976. The US CDC believed that a swine flu epidemic was imminent. It organized a massive campaign during which 46 million people took swine flu vaccine, but the epidemic never occurred. Not one person died from the disease, but several dozen died and several hundred suffered side-effects from the vaccine. In the US government's post-mortem on the incident, researchers concluded that 'since research has not yet found a good predictor of virulence, one may have no means to establish in advance the severity of a presumed pandemic'.

The bottom line is that epidemic risk managers do not talk about quantitative risk appetite – or even risk appetite at all. It is possible to have a general idea of frequency. It appears that there are cycles of pandemic flu driven by fluctuating levels of population immunity, as generations that were exposed and gained immunity die out, and the speed at which the flu virus's genes mutate. In practice it is impossible to act on this knowledge, since the timing is very vague and they would not know the exact organism in any case. Severity is equally unpredictable.

In the face of this uncertainty, risk appetite appears to be a societal construct set implicitly through support for public health funding and restrictions on civil liberties, for example mandatory quarantine. This support lags events as our perception of risk rises and falls: during an outbreak, we write a blank cheque (for example in June 2005 the Canadian state of Ontario presented the Federal government with a bill for close to C$1 billion for SARS-related costs); after an outbreak, we increase budgets; after several calm years, we don't object as budgets are pared back.

The current debate on H5N1 avian flu illustrates this collective, intangible decision-making process on the upswing. We have become aware of a substantial risk. Our governments are anxious to be seen to be doing something in response. Consequently they are noisily stockpiling Tamiflu despite weak evidence of its utility and the near-certainty that, as Fielding puts it, 'if Tamiflu were used prophylactically, the virus would end up resistant'. If the pandemic doesn't materialize and our interest in the topic wanes, our support for the measures taken to date will surely wane too.

Planning is then based on the available support for funding and intervention rather than some absolute level of risk tolerance. This lagged process is not necessarily irrational. Infectious diseases such as SARS and avian flu are not in fact the gravest health threats we face right now, even if it sometimes feels that way. Griffiths observes that many victims of SARS and avian flu already had weak immune systems through poverty or old age. Given this, she emphasizes that 'the risks of SARS and avian flu are real, but the risk of dying from a non-communicable disease [such as cancer] is much greater… in addition you have HIV… you have to balance the risks of poverty with those of disease'. McGeer is also intensely aware of the need to maintain perspective. 'Even during SARS, the risk was not like being in a war – or even being an electric lineman[2].' '[What we went through] was no worse than what people deal with in refugee camps on a daily basis. It was possible to apply a degree of grounding – it wasn't HIV, cholera in India, that kind of thing.'

If the next threat is unknowable and unquantifiable, the standard process of deriving risk management plans from a known, quantified risk appetite won't work. As long as research, containment, communications and

---

[2] Electric linemen repair electricity transmission cables. Apparently this is the most dangerous occupation in Canada.

surveillance capabilities are maintained above some minimum threshold, flexing funding levels with the perceived threat level and responding rapidly when the threat level changes would seem sensible. It would at least avoid building the epidemiological equivalent of the Maginot Line. Since 'you cannot be completely prepared for every possible infectious disease threat', according to Rau:

> you focus on the most likely threat. Right now, the focus of planning is on a respiratory pathogen that is highly contagious in incipient phases and highly secondarily infectious. However, we need to be flexible as we don't know if this will be flu, avian flu, SARS or something else. We're trying to provide a continuum of defence rather than a magic bullet against one threat.

Fielding agrees. He is sanguine about the prospects for SARS and avian flu:

> An avian flu pandemic is a relatively improbable event but the consequences are so awful that – no pun intended – everyone is running around like headless chickens... some of my physician colleagues see [our situation] as five minutes to midnight. I'm less worried since problems arise where you don't expect them; they come from behind your back. A lot of thought went into preventing oil spills at Prudeau Bay in Alaska, but no one foresaw the set of apparently mundane circumstances that led to the *Exxon Valdez* accident. Hong Kong is expecting avian flu: all chickens are vaccinated, there is a high level of biosurveillance, and all imports are from licensed farms and through licensed channels. Of course, some people were hospitalised [with avian flu]... because they'd smuggled in a cheap chicken... and what's happening in Indonesia now is very worrying.

Let us summarize, then, the process of managing the risk of unknown infectious diseases. *Doing*, not *thinking*, is the core of the process. *Doing* consists of five elements: characterize and understand the disease, creating treatment protocols and if possible a vaccine; contain the outbreak by isolating patients and protecting HCWs; communicate the risks and required behaviours to the public and HCWs; create surveillance and detection mechanisms to provide early warning of future outbreaks; and to the extent possible, influence the upstream ecosystem that supports the disease. All five of these elements embed the feedback loop from *doing* to *thinking* through the scientific peer review and publishing system.

Thinking about the risk of unknown infectious diseases is a reactive, collective and implicit process. It is reactive in that a society sets its risk appetite in response to recent outbreaks. The more recent and more severe the outbreak, the lower the risk appetite (and the stronger the link from *doing* back to *thinking*). It is collective and implicit in that this appetite is expressed indirectly through tolerance of public health spending, rather than as an explicit statement of risk tolerance.

Planning around this risk appetite is then the process of matching the available resources to the highest priority actions required to manage the risk. The lower the risk appetite, the greater the spend, and thus the greater the opportunity to research the disease, communicate with the public, change upstream behaviours and implement early warning measures. Similarly, the lower the risk appetite, the greater the tolerance for restrictions on civil liberties that assist containment.

THREAT LEVEL INCREASING

Underpinning this reactive approach is a strong implicit assumption: that the underlying level of threat is more or less constant. However, if the threat level is increasing, then the minimum capability level maintained in the troughs between epidemics may not be adequate. In the decades after the Second World War, the Nobel laureate Joshua Lederberg foresaw exactly this result. Over the past decade the writer Laurie Garrett has repeatedly highlighted the rising threat from infectious diseases. In 1998, the US CDC also acknowledged the risks. In a document called *Preventing Emerging Infectious Diseases: A strategy for the 21st Century* (1998) it noted, 'Societal, technological, and environmental factors continue to have a dramatic effect on infectious diseases worldwide, facilitating the emergence of new diseases and the re-emergence of old ones, sometimes in drug-resistant forms.'

There are four reasons that the long-term trend might be worsening. First, as noted above, the absolute numbers of cohabiting humans and domestic animals are unprecedented. This creates a fertile environment for viruses to cross species barriers. Second, equally unprecedented urbanization and the ubiquity of cross-border travel have increased contagion rates and reduced the time available to respond to an emerging threat.

Third, rising human population has led to steady encroachment into new habitats, which in turn has led to exposure to increasingly novel viruses. Researchers believe that human invasion of primate habitat on the fringes of the African rainforest led to simian immunodeficiency virus (SIV) becoming HIV. HIV is the precursor of acquired immune deficiency syndrome (AIDS), the cause of some 8,000 deaths a day in 2004. In parallel, a set of severe haemorrhagic viruses has crossed from primates to humans in Africa, including Ebola, Marburg virus, West Nile fever, and Lassa fever. A similar process appears to be underway in the Amazonian rainforest, with the discovery in recent years of Brazilian and Venezuelan haemorrhagic fevers.

Fourth, while the large-scale introduction of antibiotics, pesticides and vaccines during the 20th century killed many disease-causing organisms, it also created a super-heated evolutionary environment promoting genetic resistance to these very compounds. As a result, we see the steady appearance of strains of disease-causing microorganisms that are resistant to one or more of our standard disease control tools, such as the W-strain of tuberculosis and methicillin-resistant *Staphylococcus aureus* (MRSA).

There is an intriguing parallel in forest fire fighting. Responding to a wave of destructive fires, the US government set up the US Forest Service in 1905. One of its aims was to eliminate fire in the forests. This succeeded for some time, but by the 1980s uncontrollable fires had become more frequent. Instead of frequent small fires that burnt only the undergrowth, fire fighters encountered infrequent massive fires that destroyed entire trees and forests. A particularly bad fire season in Yellowstone National Park in 1988 marked a turning point. The Forest Service realized that fire is a critical part of a healthy forest ecosystem. Suppression was merely deferral. It has now changed its practices (see the next chapter). Human intervention produced an illusory 'success' that lasted for about 80 years. However, the intervention ended up producing the very thing it was supposed to control, in this case massive forest fires.

The US Surgeon General declared in 1967 that 'the time has come to close the book on infectious diseases. We have basically wiped out infection in the US.' If, as suggested above, our successes against infectious disease over the past century have been merely temporary, in the coming decades it may be due for as harsh a reappraisal as the 'conquest' of forest fires. While we are not helpless in the fight against infectious disease, we may simply have deferred a problem and not solved it.

APPLICATION TO BUSINESS

Contagion is relevant in risk managing portfolios of financial assets. No company is an island: the financial health of any company is dependent on the financial health of other companies. For example, in the automotive industry there is often a very close network of relationships between suppliers and auto makers. In retail too there are close relationships between manufacturers and retailers. As the financial health of an auto maker such as General Motors (GM) worsens, so does that of their major suppliers, such as Delphi. Similarly, the health of suppliers of telecommunications network equipment such as Nortel, Alcatel, Ericsson and Lucent suffered after the telecommunications bubble burst and major customers such as Worldcom and Global Crossing went bust.

If companies are grouped together in a conglomerate, problems in one area of the group may impact in another area, even if it is in a different industry. For example, GM had to sell its profitable finance arm GMAC to raise the cash to address problems in its core manufacturing business. This is especially so in cases where the details of the conglomerate structure are not transparent, as happens in emerging markets such as Mexico or Russia (or, a generation ago, in Japan).

Another type of contagion is possible when a diverse group of investors agree strongly on market outlook and end up owning similar positions. If this happens, then what seem to be quite diverse markets and assets on the surface are vulnerable to contagious price declines if this consensus changes, especially if the underlying assets are illiquid, such as small-cap stocks, exotic derivatives or emerging market equities.

This happened in the emerging markets sector in 1997. Many investors had bought into the idea that emerging markets were coming of age, and had borrowed widely in dollars to buy Brazilian, Thai, Indonesian, Russian and other emerging market equities in local currency. In mid-1997, this consensus started to crack when Thailand stopped fighting speculative attacks on its fixed exchange rate and floated the baht. The value of the baht collapsed, taking the value of baht investments with it. Dollar debts lost no value, however. As the value of investors' local currency assets approached the value of their dollar debts, they had to sell. In a vicious circle, the more assets they sold, the more asset prices fell, and the closer they got to insolvency, so the more assets they had to sell. Once they had sold the Thai assets, they had to sell the Indonesian assets, causing their prices to decline too. From Indonesia to Hong Kong, Korea, the Philippines and eventually Russia and Brazil, each market collapsed successively as investors decided that emerging markets were submerging. While there were few material economic links between the economies of the countries affected, investors' beliefs and behaviours created one – a channel for contagion.

Managing the risk of such highly connected portfolios can benefit from the application of concepts from epidemic risk management. For example, the likelihood of infectious disease transmission between two people is related to the closeness of their relationship. The likelihood of financial contagion is also the result of proximity between two companies. If you can identify links between companies, and estimate their strength, you will be able to construct portfolios that are less susceptible to contagion, or at least to hedge some of the effects. Similarly, if you know how contagion will occur, you can set up surveillance to obtain early warning of problems to come. If your warning is earlier than your competitors', you have a chance to act before they do, for example by reducing exposure or hedging.

The concepts of epidemic risk management are also relevant in some areas of operational risk. For low-frequency, high-severity events, a collective, reactive and implicit process may be an efficient way of thinking about the problem. Rather than trying to model the unmodellable and plan for every possible event, an organization could choose instead to invest in and practise general crisis management processes, maintain a large contingency fund, and buy insurance. (Buying insurance is the equivalent of public health authorities relying on the government to provide extra cash in a crisis.) This of course assumes a stable level of operational risk over the medium term.

The most obvious example of this is the management of epidemics themselves. Operational risk managers should avail themselves of the exact same paradigm of thinking, planning and doing as public health officials.

Another application is in public relations (PR) crisis management. Rather than try to imagine and then plan for every possible reputational event, the general process – who responds, what they say, what the internal process is – is specified and rehearsed, and contingency funds are set aside. According to a senior PR crisis manager, after the Asian crisis in 1997 several developing countries proactively developed public relations contingency plans.

Another possible approach based on a collective risk appetite is to rely on the government to pick up the pieces afterwards. If your firm is a very large financial institution that might be considered 'too big to fail', then this might just be a viable strategy. Adopting this strategy would be an illustration of moral hazard, where the risk takers are separated from the consequences of their actions, and the existence of protection encourages increased risk taking. This is the antithesis of risk management.

Some of these themes will recur in the next chapter, where we examine the risk management of wildfires.

2

Wildfire

Interviewees

Marc Castellnou	Head of fire management strategy, Forest Fire Service, Interior Ministry, Catalonia, Spain
Paul de Mar	Head of research at Forestry Commission, New South Wales, Australia
Mike Nation	Head of Department of Forestry and Fire Prevention, California, USA
Steve Taylor	Head of fire research, Forest Fire Service, Canada
Nick Collins	Head of strategic risk management, London Fire Brigade
Adam Kleczkowski	Lecturer in mathematical biology at University of Cambridge, UK
Tim Eldridge	Former smokejumper, Montana, USA
Bill Moody	Former smokejumper, California, USA

Marc Castellnou, the head of fire management strategy at the Catalan Forest Fire Service, has a history with fire that dates back to 1981, when he was 11 years old:

> We went to work on a new fire that was burning the remaining half of the 48,000 hectares of forest in [my home] territory. We trapped it and we felt the pleasure of victory. It was the last time that I would see the forest that I knew as a child. From this moment until just recently I felt as if we had lost the paradise where we grew up, learnt to know the trees and the birds, and listen to the wind.

In 1983, aged 13, Castellnou learnt to fear fire. 'A fire trapped us. My grandfather said to us, "Today's a good day to die", as he taught me,

Jordi and Miquel to make a fire hole.' In 1989, he played the lead role in a fire fight:

> It was *la gran castanya* [the real deal]. A lightning fire burned at night. In the morning we went to work but the fire went into alignment [had slope, wind and aspect in its favour.] For a while we contained it, but that day produced a generational change. Jordi and I had to rescue our parents from the fire. We were already faster and we knew enough about fire. We put out the front [of the fire] with a counter-fire when 15 truckloads of fire fighters couldn't. We tasted victory and public recognition, but we also saw how our country was full of brush but not trees.

That is, all the full-grown trees had burnt down in successive fires and only brush remained. The forest that Castellnou had known as a child had disappeared.

In 1994 a fire changed his life:

> I was in a massive fire, trying to be a good soldier. I lost four friends and started a journey [to find out why]. Now I've understood why my friends died. Not because we didn't do enough but because through misfortune they were in the wrong place at the wrong time... and they thought they were superheros but [in reality] had no training. I have often wanted to think that if I had been there with them, they would have got out. But it's not true: I would have died with them.
>
> I was already 10 metres away, in a safe area [that had already been burned over]... because I smelt the warning of conflagration, the gases of pyrolysis, and felt the calm at the eye of the storm. I ran away and escaped from the fire... because if I [had] learnt one thing it was to be afraid, to fear that element that had gobbled up my universe. For this reason I survived and they didn't.

After the tragedy, Castellnou found local fire fighting wanting, and looked for other answers. He went to the United States to study and gained a PhD in fire management. Interviewed in late 2005 in Catalonia he describes how, on his return, he 'built a database of all the fires in the region over the past 50 years. It is better than simulation, it is real. Look at this area here', he says, pointing at the map on his laptop screen.

> You see there have been three fires in the same place? This one happened in 1949, this one in 1970 and this one in 2000. You see how the shape is the same each time – but the area burnt gets bigger and bigger. And here, you see these photos: the only parts of the forest to survive the big burn in 2000 were those parts that had experienced smaller burns since 1970. If

the fuel is scarce the fire only scorches the trunk; if it's abundant, it burns the crown and then the trees die, for ever.

Castellnou has found what he was looking for. It wasn't what he expected. 'Now, 11 years on, I've got a PhD. I've simulated and modelled everything. I've concluded that we should do what my grandparents did: let the fires burn.'

Castellnou has an easy laugh and a starburst of smile lines around his eyes, but he doesn't laugh or smile when he talks about fire:

> A former head of the [Catalan] forest fire service said 'I'm here to protect nature from itself.' Well, this is what you get. Nature needs to be protected from us, not from itself. We try to put all the fires out, and all that happens is that they get bigger and bigger because there's so much fuel. A forest without fire is not pure or pristine: it's sterile, already dead. Why do we want to return to a past that was never there anyway?

Paul de Mai is head of research at the New South Wales (NSW) Forestry Commission. He agrees that fire suppression by itself is doomed. 'It's a dam burst scenario: eventually you'll get overwhelmed when multiple fires break out in dry weather ahead of a storm.' Unlike Castellnou though, he feels that the challenge is to keep catastrophes in mind and protect against them, even as they fail to materialize year after year, rather than to let the fires burn:

> Fires here are on a long cycle of 30 years – we had major fires in 2003, 1968 and 1939 – with a subcycle of four to seven years. Since a plantation needs 30 years to mature, the trees have to survive at least one big fire season and lots of small ones. It only takes a single fire event to cause a lot of damage. The fire fighters in Canberra thought they were doing a good job since they hadn't lost a house in 50 years... then in 2003, a fire burned 10,500 hectares, and caused a loss of A$66 million.

He continues:

> In 1983 'Ash Wednesday', the largest fire event in Australian history, destroyed 23,000 hectares, and caused a loss of A$100–200 million. You think you've eliminated the risk... then Old Father Time catches up with you and you lose 500 houses in an afternoon. We try to optimize our fire management... [but] the problem is that we see the cost every day but the benefits once every 30 years. No one stays at an organization for 30 years these days. I was talking to a mentor the other day and he said to me 'Paul, don't you worry about the 10-year fires, it's the 100-year fire that'll catch you out.'

NATURAL FIRE LOADS

Forests in hot, dry environments have evolved to tolerate and even exploit fire. For example, Ponderosa pines, native to the Rocky Mountains and widely distributed in the west and south-west of the United States, can tolerate mild fires since they have thick bark, deep roots, few low branches and a high crown. They exploit fires since the fires incinerate competing saplings. In addition, downstream waterways depend on forests to retain water after a rainfall. If they do not, the waterways end up clogged with silt. Over long periods of time, such ecosystems reach equilibrium, with stable long-term fire frequencies and severities.

This equilibrium risk level is the foundation for thinking about risk in this environment. In addition, fire managers select a risk appetite for fire management operations. Despite his attachment to the forest, Castellnou states bluntly that 'All the forests in Catalonia are not worth a single fire fighter. Our risk appetite is zero casualties.'

FIRE SEASON PLANNING

The first step in *planning* in this environment is to estimate the forests' inherent fire risk level. In California, Mike Nation's Department of Forestry and Fire Prevention coordinates and quality controls the development of California's annual fire plan based on input from local fire units.

Prior to the season, his department combines the local plans from each of California's 21 fire units. Each unit assesses the local fire threat, based on three components: fuel, weather and terrain. Over time, the accumulation and growth of fuel such as grass, brush or slash (residue left on the ground after logging) can reinforce prolonged dry periods to increase both fire size and frequency. Certain terrain types, particularly steep-sided valleys, both make control harder and act as a natural funnel for wind, increasing potential severity.

All the plans are seasoned with 100 years of accumulated California fire knowledge and collectively published as *The Blue Book*. They are also used as the baseline for fire simulation models which predict fire frequency and severity profiles (see box below). These predictions drive the budget request. Nation notes that 'If the [season's] prognosis is bad, we request emergency funds for the contingency account.'

The long-term trend is that fires in California, as in the rest of the United States, are getting bigger and more frequent. California's fire management strategy document laments that 'once thought of as a seasonal hazard, wildfires are an almost everyday occurrence in California'. Some of this is the hangover from 50 years of fire suppression. In addition Nation believes that disease has weakened the forest, killing trees and providing fuel. He finds the situation today a 'Catch-22: lots of rain means lots of fuel; no rain means easier ignition'. Climate change may be playing a role, by changing rainfall patterns and extending the range of tree parasites. Whatever the cause, the natural frequency and severity of fires are at a historical high and they may yet increase further, causing ongoing serious problems as California's population grows and human habitation steadily encroaches on the forests.

Based on their understanding of current fire risks, fire managers trade off different, often conflicting, objectives. For example, forests provide timber, recreational space and wildlife habitat. Maximizing timber yield makes for ugly, unnatural forests; maximizing recreational space disturbs animals; maximizing wildlife habitat is best achieved by excluding humans entirely. This trade-off is a political process, and its outcome will depend on the balance of forces for development, exploitation and conservation.

Whatever their objective, prior to the fire season, fire managers can influence the frequency and severity of fires. The most common practices are to reduce fuel loads by removing brush and to create fire obstacles such as fire breaks. They can also intervene more directly in the ecosystem by changing vegetation mix through grazing, selective pruning and planting, and by setting fires deliberately – a practice known as controlled burning.

CONTROLLED BURNS

Castellnou is a strong advocate of controlled burning:

> Right now in the good years the fire fighters sit around doing nothing. In the bad years they are overwhelmed. What we should do is take advantage of the good years to set controlled fires so that in the bad years we don't lose control. In the winters, when people are worried about Christmas presents and mortgage payments, we should set fires.

This strategy trades off increased frequency in return for reduced severity. Since flexible resource allocation is required for such a strategy, Castellnou doesn't want to be given specific items of equipment that may or may not prove useful:

We need [a sum of money] per hectare protected that I can use as I want, not an allocation of so many fire fighters, so many trucks, helicopters and so on. I want to be able to reallocate funds between fire prevention and fire extinction according to the need rather than be tied down to a fixed resource base just because it sounds good in Parliament.

Steve Taylor, the head of fire research at the Canadian Forest Fire Service, is also open to the idea of controlled burning. He notes that:

In the United States there's an attitudinal dimension: not quite 'put the fire out at all costs', but close. Maybe because we have a lower population density – most of the time 'it's only trees' out there – in Canada fire management is more conservative. We're less likely to put fire fighters at risk... we've had few fatalities. We also have [fewer] smokejumpers, although we do have helicopter-trained crews.

There isn't a policy of putting out every fire everywhere. It wouldn't make sense economically or ecologically to fight every fire. Agencies are recognizing that there's an economic limit [on what they can do], and they are modifying their responses. In Quebec, for example, they've designated a line of latitude, and on one side something's done [about a fire] and on the other side nothing's done. In British Columbia there's no line but policy is becoming more explicit.

In Canada's national parks, the idea of letting fires burn is positively mainstream. 'Wood Buffalo Park in Alberta... [is] very remote, almost entirely wilderness... they basically don't fight fires. In Banff National Park there's a fairly active programme which started in 1975. The [steep] topography provides some control since fires can't move easily.' Park authorities use sophisticated fire simulation models to predict fire development (see below), but they tend to show that the fire will burn itself out if left alone. As a precaution, the rangers burn out valleys so that the fire can't spread outside the park or into the town. Over time, these forests should revert to their long-run equilibrium state, climate change permitting.

However, Taylor admits that parks are still exceptional:

There hasn't been a big constituency for [controlled burning], outside natural parks. We're in a time when it is recognized as a useful tool, but it's not used that widely. Every land management agency has a policy that permits its use, but actual use varies. In areas that are remote it's easier to let natural fires burn. In areas that are more developed it's different.

There are too many properties at stake simply to let fires burn.

De Mar says that 'We are the major practitioner of prescribed burning in the state. [That said] there are not many areas where we use deliberate burning.' He defines controlled burning narrowly:

> If a fire accumulates under relatively mild conditions, the area is remote, and there are no adverse weather conditions forecast, then we might decide to bring it to its logical boundaries. We would then [set artificial fires to] burn out the fuel within a perimeter by burning back from trails and ridges.

Interestingly, there is a partial parallel with urban fire fighting. The London Fire Brigade (LFB) has concluded that responding to a fire is the last resort, 'the least effective way to save lives', according to Nick Collins, LFB's head of strategic risk management. 'We could reduce the number of fires without reducing the number of deaths', he says, as deaths tend to be concentrated in a few, severe fires. Consequently, most of the strategic efforts are focused on protection, 'buying time for people to escape' with smoke alarms, fire doors and sprinklers. As in forests, the LFB finds that rushing to put out every fire is less useful than trying to address the underlying drivers of damage. Unlike forest fire fighters, of course, it is primarily concerned about human loss of life rather than trees.

FIGHTING FIRES

After the man-made fire season comes the God-given one. During the fire season, Nation's department acts as the state clearing house for all fire management information and resources. Based in two operational centres, and working closely with the National Weather Service, the team monitors temperature, humidity, recovery rate (the change in humidity between night and day), fuel build-up and wind event patterns in each area. Feedback from local teams is also captured. This information creates a rich picture of fires and fire risks.

This rich picture is used to allocate resources. Through the California Master Mutual Aid Agreement (MMAA: see Chapter 9 on earthquakes for more detail), Nation's office can control all the fire-fighting equipment in the state. The MMAA is a state-wide legal agreement that pools all equipment regardless of its owner, and specifies who is responsible for doing what under what circumstances. Through satellite monitoring devices – relatives of high end anti-theft car tracking devices such as LoJack® – the team knows the location of every piece of fire equipment in the state in real time. Nation's team aims to employ the 'closest resource, regardless of the colour of the fire engine'. As the risk level increases, they pre-position equipment and crews where they will be needed, and update crew work schedules to ensure staff availability.

Money is not usually an issue in the short term. Nation observes that:

> There are very variable demands on budget due to the weather. On a bad day, several hundred fires might start over a 24-hour period. In most cases we can request extra money. In the short term there are no monetary limitations, it's more [the scarcity of] people and materials. It's always a question of resource allocation – how do we best assess the risk to things that matter [and protect them]?

De Mar describes a similar process in New South Wales. There is a legal framework for resource sharing through the Rural Fires Act. This Act governs the fire-fighting roles and responsibilities of four agencies: the volunteer rural fire service, the professional NSW fire brigade, the Forestry Commission, and the National Parks and Wildlife Service.

Operationally there are also close parallels. 'Each day we get the fire danger index from the Weather Bureau', explains De Mar. 'The Weather Bureau predicts the temperature, the dryness and the wind and combines the results in the index. Depending on the index we have different readiness levels. If it's at the highest level', his teams will take up a preventive stance. 'We'll have employees on fire trucks in the bush; we'll stop harvesting, since that creates a fire hazard; we'll close plantations to the public; and we'll pre-position equipment like bulldozers.'

Modelling fire

Once a fire is burning, fire managers track it, sometimes putting 'spotters' in place to keep an eye on it, either on the ground or from the air. The progress of each fire is logged and captured in a database. The database, which ideally contains the full fire history of the region, feeds simulation models which predict the fire's behaviour given the current conditions. Fire managers plan the fire fight using these predictions.

Such models are related to models of epidemic spread. Indeed, the first generation of epidemic spread models were adapted from forest fire models, according to Dr Adam Kleczkowski, lecturer in mathematical biology at the University of Cambridge, they share the concept of something spreading from neighbour to neighbour in proportion to distance, in this case sparks rather than microorganisms.

Fires require fuel, ignition and air. If a fire has plentiful fuel, once it has started wind is the major factor behind its progress. In Catalonia, Castellnou's historical database shows that fires on the coast in the summer tend to make a 90-degree turn inland during course of the day. This is because the wind direction moves steadily throughout the day. Other patterns also emerge from historical analysis. In Catalonia, says Castellnou:

> Although the intensity [of the fire] varies there are 14 patterns… basically 14 combinations of terrain and weather. We have a pre-defined management strategy for each pattern. Knowing this makes a big difference to how you position your fire fighters. Before this analysis, every fire appeared new.

Combined with data on terrain and vegetation type, local weather history, and the simulation of fire dynamics and wind, these models are powerful tools for planning both overall fire strategy and tactics for fighting individual fires.

A particular complication of fire modelling is that very intense fires make their own wind. Pointing at a video playing on his laptop, Castellnou explains another aspect of fire behaviour. 'You see the way that pillar of smoke is inclined? It looks like there's a strong wind.' He points to another, smaller smoke plume.

> But look over there, there was no wind on this day. Fires with enough fuel… create a feedback loop where the hot air produced at the centre of the fire rises and cools, but is then sucked back into the base. This kind of fire can throw fire brands hundreds of metres ahead and move far faster than fire fighters. The fire takes control of the situation.

The knowledge that fires can move fast even without wind is critical to correctly positioning fire fighters. Similarly:

> It is possible to use the fire's 'respiration' against it. If you set counter-fires intelligently, you can both drag it in the direction you want and reduce the fuel available. The fire drags itself towards the fires you set, but when it gets there, there's no fuel left.

Extinguishing a fire by forcing it to burn itself out is called entrapment. This is what Castellnou was referring to in the opening paragraph of this chapter.

> Castellnou shows another clip, this time of a mushroom cloud rising menacingly into a clear blue sky. The hairs on the back of your neck stand up:
>
> > The worst situation – a firestorm – occurs when you have a large fire during a drought and a cold front approaches. See here: the smoke rises and hits the incoming cold, moist air. It cools rapidly, forming this mushroom cloud. The cloud becomes heavier than the air below it and collapses on top of the fire. You get uncontrolled spread in all directions. When I saw this, I evacuated 600 fire fighters immediately. Three minutes later, there was a firestorm.

SMOKEJUMPING

At the sharp end of the fire managers' predictions and strategies – *doing* – are the fire fighters. Tim Eldridge was a wildland fire fighter and 'smokejumper'– an elite fire fighter who parachutes into remote fires – for 15 years. Although dozens of fires can occur in a single day:

> Most are small. Ninety-nine per cent are caused by lightning. We send crews of two to four people to tackle them. The risks are that you get injured jumping in, or that the fire escalates. To manage this, each job is subject to job hazard analysis while the crew is still in the air. The analysis covers weather, topography, fuel amount and type, and possible safe areas and escape routes. The incident commander directs the process.

For larger fires, fire managers initiate a formal incident management system. (In California, this is the Standard Emergency Management System (SEMS), as described in Chapter 9.)

Eldridge notes that 'smokejumpers receive extensive training, but the field is very different from the classroom'. He found out quite how different when in July 1981 he fought a fire on the Salmon River in Central Idaho. With accuracy characteristic of someone whose life depended on paying close attention to temperature, wind, humidity and dry vegetation on steep slopes, 25 years later he recalls:

> It was 93 to 100 degrees [Fahrenheit] with minimal wind, but very dry. It was dangerous terrain: Ponderosa pine, brush, open grassy hillsides, steep-sided valleys with 55 to 70 per cent gradients. The kind of terrain where you'd get chased all over the place by fire. We were in a crew of 20, with an inexperienced leader.

We rode in a helicopter to the top of the ridge, then walked towards the fire. We peeled off the side of the ridge, following the edge of the fire. On the second day, everything was going smoothly, then the supervisor ordered us to dig a fire line [a break in vegetation created by fire fighters as a barrier to fire movement] down the hill and light backfires into the fire. That was an absolute no-no, a red flag – we couldn't see the fire below us, and you don't go down a hill if you can't see below you. The fire was coming up the slope, I could hear it roaring. I told the supervisor we had to move. He said 'No, keep going.' Me and another team leader pulled our people out. We walked back up the hill to the black [burnt area]. I was thinking, this is really stupid – the fire is below us, this is steep country, you shouldn't give up the high ground.

By the time the rest caught up with us they were running for their lives. The fire had moved below us in a J-shape, and become more like a U. We were in the middle of the U. We didn't have a good lookout position, so we couldn't see the fire. We didn't have any communications with the bottom of the valley. The supervisor was written up and reprimanded.

Bill Moody, also a smokejumper for 33 years, elaborates why a reprimand was necessary:

Fire fighters should only descend a slope towards a fire in very exceptional circumstances; otherwise you should always start from an anchor point at the heel [rear] of the fire. Fire fighters need a good understanding of fire behaviour: the interaction of fuel, weather, and wind.

In addition:

They need to be aware of changes in conditions, especially wind, and change their tactical positioning accordingly. Fire crews are trained to identify safety zones and [escape] routes to them. As a last resort they have the fire shelter. It's a small tent weighing about four and a half pounds. It's saved a number of lives.

As unbelievable as this sounds, when about to be overtaken by a fire, fire fighters scrape bare a tent-sized area on the ground, deploy the tent and lie still while the fire burns over them.

Moody too knows of what he speaks:

On 16 July 1984 I led a team of 20 smokejumpers from the North Cascades Smokejumper Base in North Central Washington on a fire just north of the US–British Columbia border. The fire was burning in the Merritt District on British Columbia Forest Service land just north of the United States Pasayten Wilderness Area. We were called in because the fire was within a few miles of the United States and predicted to cross the border.

As the first jumper team arrived on scene the 400-acre fire was picking up intensity. We dropped our streamers [wind indicators] over a safe spot about 800 metres from the heel [rear] of the fire. The streamers indicated about 200 metres of [lateral] drift [on the way down]. We flew our jump run – my partner and I exited – and just then the fire made a major run, going from about 400 acres to 600–800 acres. The effect was to create a major indraft towards the fire... sucking us in at about 15 miles per hour. On the way down my jump partner and I were just looking for alternate landing areas and hoping we wouldn't be sucked into the fire – and praying. Instead of travelling 200 horizontal metres during the 90-second descent we travelled over 1,000, landing on the fire perimeter at the heel of the fire. Luckily it had pretty much burnt out by then. Had we selected a different landing site lateral to the middle or upper part of the fire [we could have been sucked into the fire and] it could have been fatal.

Later in his career Moody became involved in aerial fire fighting. He notes that it's not just the fire that's dangerous. 'One hundred and fifty people have died in air tankers [in fire-fighting operations] since 1955. The airspace above a fire can be a hazardous environment as well... requiring strict control and coordination.'

Apart from the fire itself, the presence of property complicates fire management. Owners of properties with unblemished forest views do not want to be told that their property is not worth saving, nor that it's collateral damage from a controlled burn that escaped control, as has happened several times in the United States in recent years. For example, in 2000 fire fighters lost control of a prescribed burn near Los Alamos in New Mexico. It burned several thousand acres and over 200 houses. 'If a fire is near homes... we'll throw a lot more resources at it', says de Mar. Eldridge notes that 'development on the forest fringes has become very politically sensitive. This can distract from overall fire strategy, which can be costly: we focus on saving property rather than minimizing the overall damage.'

The apparent success of fire suppression over the past 80 years has reduced public perceptions of risk. As in the management of other natural disasters such as floods, this has led to moral hazard, where the public assumes that someone else will protect them from risk, even as they take increasing levels of it. Moreover, the fire risk is now increasing. Expect tension to increase.

SUMMARY

Fundamentally, the only way to eliminate fire completely from many forests would be to concrete them over. Trying to shape the system to our ends using fire control has not been successful. US Forest Service (USFS) official figures show both the acreage burnt and the likelihood of large fires increasing steadily from about 1980. The Federal Wildland Fire Management Policy of 2003 includes the following frank admission:

> Today, after a century of fire exclusion, extensive areas of the country are at risk from intense, severe wildfires that threaten nearby communities, burn well beyond the adaptive limits of the wildlands, and cause significant [ecological damage].

Eldridge observes that 'fire's been around longer than we have; so have forests. Fire keeps the forest healthy. It's a natural occurrence.' Different forests have different fundamental fire capacities. They do the *thinking* for us. In remote, undeveloped national parks it is possible to let fires burn. However, in most developed areas the clock can't be turned back. Fires cannot be left alone to burn the forest back to a sustainable state. This is the result partly of fire suppression, and possibly climate change; deforming forest ecosystems to the point where they have become vast tinderboxes, and partly of the fact that it would be politically impossible to let houses and timber plantations burn. These unintended consequences may foreshadow the way in which our intervention in another natural ecosystem – man and its microbial predators (see the previous chapter) – may play out. What seemed like a good idea at the time may worsen the situation in the long term.

In these cases, risk managers have to balance potential economic and ecological losses, and their own risk appetite. *Planning* is the process of making these trade-offs. It starts with calculating the fire capacity of the forest at a given moment in time – it is bigger after a drought, for instance. Fire managers use this information to set a balance between conflicting goals: fire fighters' safety, timber yields, habitat, recreational land and property protection, and (increasingly) carbon emissions. The objective drives resource requirements and out-of-season fire management such as controlled burning. During the fire season, these resources are arrayed pre-emptively against emerging fire threats. *Doing* then involves devising a management plan for a specific fire and fighting it. Each year the loop from *doing* back to *thinking* and *planning* is closed as the weather patterns and operational experiences of the fire season are added to the historical record.

APPLICATION TO BUSINESS

Best practice portfolio risk management at large financial institutions mirrors the process of regional fire management planning and doing, albeit on a smaller scale and a higher level of detail. Like a regional fire manager, a portfolio manager sets the overall risk appetite for his or her portfolio. The portfolio manager communicates this to subordinate sub-portfolio managers.

Like the local fire managers, each sub-portfolio manager assesses the risks and conditions locally – problem areas, structural risks, long-term trends and the impact of the overall environment – and decides which risks the institution can tolerate and which risks it wants to mitigate. He or she then reports the results upwards to the portfolio manager. The overall portfolio manager adds up all the sub-portfolio inputs, combines it with historic and forecast macroeconomic conditions, simulates possible outcomes, and creates an overall portfolio risk profile and management plan. He or she uses the profile to allocate resources and set performance expectations. Higher potential gains mean bigger budgets; higher risks mean more resources for risk management, which often even involves 'fire fighting'. Portfolio managers can take pre-emptive action to reduce the portfolio risk, such as reallocating funds between areas, selling or hedging assets.

As the financial year evolves, problems arise with different assets and asset classes. Sub-portfolio managers develop a detailed plan to address each problem, which they then execute, taking care to assess the reaction of the market to their actions. Plans range from aggressive withdrawal (that is, selling stocks) to aggressive attack, for example leading a shareholder revolt against management. After each cycle, portfolio managers incorporate the lessons learnt into their models and policies for ongoing use. This process maps well to fire management practices.

If forest fires break out and are repeatedly suppressed, the forest as a whole gets weaker and the risk of catastrophic fire increases. At times, a similar process operates in credit portfolios. Rather than force customers into bankruptcy, banks will sometimes work with them to alleviate the situation. For example, they might extend the term of the loan, forgive certain fees, or even reduce the interest rate. This is especially likely if senior management has gone on record saying something like 'We don't have any bad debts, only customers in need of support', or if senior bank regulators have gone on record saying something like 'There is no bad debt problem in [country X].'

However, if the customer is simply too weak to survive, by providing support banks risk creating a steadily weaker portfolio of half-bankrupt companies. Small fires are put out but the forest is collectively weakened and the probability of a big fire increases. Arguably banks in Japan in the 1990s did just this, creating portfolios full of 'zombie' companies which only stayed in business because of repeated lightening of their financial burdens, and then sucked the life out of their fitter competitors. The economy stagnated for a decade as resources remained unproductively employed in these companies, and several large banks failed. Without significant government intervention – for example buying distressed debt for far above its market price and maintaining ultra-low interest rates – and a timely economic boom in China, more would have followed. Sometimes bankers – and regulators – should let the 'fire' consume a weak company and take the hit, otherwise they risk weakening the whole portfolio, and ultimately the whole economy.

More generally, the history of fighting fires illustrates two larger points, both of which are relevant for risk managers. First, risk management cannot eliminate risk. Although it is tempting to try, any risk management strategy that aims to eliminate risk will fail. We have to accept that the world is not under our control and that unpleasant stuff happens.

Second, the world is a complex place. As a result, simplistic solutions are prone to unexpected consequences. Smothering all fires looks like an appealing strategy to manage fire risk. However, it goes against the grain of complex forest ecosystems and their downstream dependants. It makes things worse. Most natural and human systems are more complex than they look, and risk managers should think carefully about the consequences of their actions. The more simplistic the action, the more carefully we should think about the consequences.

The next chapter takes us in a completely different direction, the management of terrorism risk.

3

Terrorism

Interviewees

Ricky Ogden	Crew manager, London Fire Brigade, UK
Eric Westropp	Head of Iraqi operations at Control Risks, UK
Anonymous	CEO, security firm, Iraq
Anonymous	Former UK commando, now security manager, Iraq
Anonymous	Former officer in the UK Special Forces
Anonymous	Lieutenant Colonel in UK Special Forces
Nick Collins	Assistant Commissioner and head of strategic risk management, London Fire Brigade, UK

Ricky Ogden, a crew manager at the London Fire Brigade (LFB), was on duty at Islington in north London when the call came in on 7 July 2005:

> At 0900 a friend said 'listen to this', and we all heard 'major incident' on the radio. They were calling the world and his aunt to the scene, all the agencies. We knew something big was going on.
>
> We were called to Aldgate at 0915. We got there at 0924, the traffic was mega-slow.[1] We heard various messages on the way but we didn't really know what [the incident] was – 'fire and explosion' was all. We thought it might be a short circuit or a train crash.
>
> As we rounded the Aldgate roundabout and drew up to the station, we realized that it was a bad situation. The first fire crew to arrive were treating people on the pavement. There was a blue light [emergency vehicle] arriving every 10 to 15 seconds. The guv'nor [team leader] said 'Stay here' and went to find the commander. He came back and told us 'A bomb's gone off. We need cutting equipment. Get down to the track.' We were really taken aback. I thought, this is really happening.

---

[1] Only someone used to driving with a flashing blue light on their roof could possibly think that 9 minutes from Islington to Aldgate during rush hour is slow.

As we went down [into the station] people were still coming up. There were lots of live casualties on the track, lots of blackened faces, blood and tears.

However, people were calm, he recalls, and there was 'no stampede'.

[On our side too] there was a surreal calmness… everyone was working together. Lots of things clicked on the day. Our interaction with other agencies was spot on, it was the slickest rescue operation I'd ever seen. The training worked, the inter-agency management was very professional. No panic, no stressing out, no shouting.

The train was about 30 to 40 metres into the tunnel. The tunnel was double width, which had dispersed some of the force. It was very quiet. It smelled of cordite, fireworks. The train doors had been blown off, so we put a ladder up.

Inside it was carnage. The device was on the floor so everyone's legs were blown off. It was the first time I'd seen blast injuries – concentrated heat and blast. Not like a car crash. A helo [helicopter] doctor turned up and prioritized the injured. He was ruthless but he had to be. Two people were still alive, six dead. I led the crew to release one of them. It was very moving. There was a lot of compassion down there – big macho fire fighters comforting dying people in their last moments.

Once the last live casualty was out it became a crime scene and we were ordered to leave. As we left the CBRN [Chemical, Bacteriological, Radiological, Nuclear] team turned up in space suits. The first officer to arrive had done a dynamic risk assessment and said there was no CBRN threat. We were all still worried about CBRN, and about a secondary device. [As we worked] I remember thinking, I hope this is like Madrid and it's conventional. Everyone was looking around, thinking the same thing. You're between a rock and a hard place though: if you use breathing apparatus it takes much longer [to get in position]. At a recent exercise in the Tube, it took us 45 minutes to get down to the platform [wearing CBRN protective clothing].

The most frightening aspect was the awareness of our own mortality. I remember walking out thinking we did a really good job, but there are no happy endings in this kind of thing. If it's CBRN, we're dead in a day.

While the terrorist bombings on 7 July 2005 were an extreme event, the London Underground is not normally an extreme environment. Many elements of Ogden's experience that day are common to all 'major incident' responses in the United Kingdom; the LFB is only one of many agencies involved. One theme of this book is that extreme environments clarify risk management. This chapter will clarify the issues of terrorism risk management through an examination of the practices of civilian and military risk managers in present-day Iraq.

IRAQ

Present-day Iraq is the most extreme environment covered in this book. Over the summer of 2006, the death toll reached 100 per day. The most conservative estimates estimate that at least 30,000 have died since the US-led invasion started in 2003. There are many groups responsible for the killings, including secular Saddam loyalists, religiously motivated Sunnis and Shias, foreign terrorists, professional hijackers, security contractors and coalition troops. Regardless of the motivation, it is clear that this is a very dangerous place. Consequently, thinking about risk in Iraq is also clear. Anyone who is uncomfortable with the constant threat of a violent death should not go; if already there, they should leave if they can. Since this option is tragically not open to most Iraqis, the discussion that follows focuses on foreigners, who have the choice to stay or leave as they wish.

For Eric Westropp, head of Iraqi operations at Control Risks, a security consulting firm, setting up operations in Iraq was 'a commercial reality. Our clients asked us to protect them [there]. It was quite controversial internally.' Once the firm had decided it would accept the risk, 'our view was that we owed a duty of care to both our clients and our employees. As an ethical choice, this means [we have] a low risk appetite.' Westropp doesn't specify how low. However, in common with other risk managers who have personally experienced extreme environments, it is apparent that Westropp, formerly a brigadier in the British Army, is aiming for no casualties at all.

In an environment with such a pervasive life and death threat, the separation between *planning* and *doing* breaks down. Risk managers in Iraq go through the *plan/do* risk management cycle repeatedly every single day. This process is not the same as planning and doing for a one in 100 year storm or epidemic.

Terrorists' foreign targets spend their time either in a base or in transit. Foreigners in Iraq do not go shopping, or to the gym, the movie theatre or anywhere else. They work, live and sleep in heavily guarded and fortified compounds. They leave only to transit to another, equally well-protected compound. Since the terrorists don't (yet) have heavy weaponry like tanks or warplanes, these bases are relatively easy to defend, so defenders have the advantage. Vehicles in transit are not as easy to fortify and defend, so attackers have the advantage. The attackers sensibly concentrate their resources on attacks on vehicles in transit. The three main strands of managing this risk are intelligence, transport tactics and equipment, and staffing. In addition, as a last resort, civilian risk managers can call on the military for support.

Intelligence-led risk management

Understanding the nature and intensity of the threat is the first step. 'We run an intelligence-based operation,' says Westropp. 'We employ a number of Iraqis to supply us with up-to-the-minute information, and at each of our [operational] sites we have trained intelligence analysts. At a minimum we can ensure that we're not surprised by demonstrations, rallies, religious celebrations, or Coalition activity.'

Intelligence can come from surprising sources:

> For example, every day one of our teams went to a certain junction and turned right. Every day our team leader waved at the newspaper seller on the corner, and every day he waved back. One day, he didn't wave back. Instead, he drew his finger across his throat. The team didn't go right, and a roadside bomb was found later.

Given the sensitivity of the situation in Iraq, many sources requested anonymity. One of them, the CEO of another security firm active in Iraq, agrees that the heart of his operation is intelligence. Specifically, he stresses the importance of reconnaissance. Ambushes in transit are most likely to occur where vehicles are in the open for a long time, slowing down, or both, since this exposes them to heavy machine gun fire. On routes his teams have never used before, they carry out detailed research beforehand, focusing on such potential ambush points. These locations are avoided if possible, and if unavoidable, security teams pass through them on heightened defensive alert. Fresh intelligence regarding threats is processed and distributed to operational teams in real time, illustrating the integration of *planning* and *doing* in this environment. Another specific issue he highlights is watching out for anyone watching over you – counter-surveillance. If people are watching you, they have plans for you.

The fundamental lesson for civilian risk managers is that if the intelligence indicates significant risk, don't leave base. As in the mountains (see Chapter 5), there is the temptation to take the risk and proceed with the mission even if the forecast is bad. In Iraq today, routinely ignoring intelligence would be suicidal. This is so central that Westropp maintains he would terminate the contract of a client who disagreed with his people's risk assessment. 'On any given tactical decision, for example whether or not to go down a certain route on a certain day, we have the last word. That's part of our contract. If a client doesn't agree with our approach, we let them go.'

Concealment versus deterrence in transit

If the clients and their security providers do decide to venture out, the next layer of risk management is to manage the risk in transit. There are two broad schools of thought: discretion to minimize visibility, or aggression to maximize deterrence.

Westropp summarizes the majority view among non-military security providers: 'We want to be low profile: we are there to protect and extract.' To that end:

> We do not undertake convoy escorting or static guarding contracts and are very discriminating about the CP [close protection, ie bodyguarding] tasks we accept. In addition we use tactics that minimize the likelihood of conflict. We use armoured [vehicles], but we're not gun-toting; we don't use suppressing fire [automatic fire directed in the general direction of the enemy to get them to keep their heads down]; and we do not conduct proactive offensive actions. We also want to be good citizens [and treat Iraqis with respect]. This works to reduce our risk.

Control Risks typically uses new, armoured, off-road-capable vehicles and armed guards, often foreign. Its vehicles are consequently relatively easy to identify. Another approach is to further lower a client's profile by attempting to blend into local traffic. The other security firm mentioned above uses a mix of personal and commercial vehicles – even a pizza delivery van in one instance – that are all local, second-hand, and discreetly armoured, if armoured at all. Clothing for employees and clients is similarly second-hand and local. Sometimes the client drives ahead in a separate vehicle with a chase car behind watching out for trouble. The downside, explains a local security manager, who also requested anonymity, is that 'There's only so low [profile] you can go. If you're in a regular car and you get attacked, you can't manoeuvre out of the situation, because you can't go over the median strip or off road.' In addition, if an attack occurs, the clients are generally better off in armoured vehicles.

Following this line of logic, other security firms take a radically different stance on transit risk management. They manage the risk through deterrence. Their vehicles are bristling with armed men and visibly armoured. They maintain an 'exclusion zone' around their vehicles, and if another car gets too close, they may immobilize it with a bullet through the engine block. While they are easy to see, so are the consequences of attacking them. Blackwater Inc, the provider of personal security to former Coalition Provisional Authority leader L Paul Bremer and the employer of the four guards killed in Fallujah (see the Preface), is the best known – but by no means the only – practitioner of this approach in Iraq.

Although Blackwater staff declined to be interviewed for this book, almost every other security professional interviewed referred to it by name. In general the reference is critical. The unnamed CEO was scathing. 'In-your-face, go-in-hard macho idiots that like the high profile and the weaponry. They think they can deter [the attackers.] You can't deter someone who's ready to die... Mike Tyson wouldn't scare Osama bin Laden.' In his view the individuals involved enjoy the adrenaline rush, and this enjoyment drives their tactics, not the needs of the clients. Equally unappealing from his point of view, this is bad for business, 'because [these] people are doing [protection] the wrong way, companies are taking casualties and pulling out'.

The same CEO is not risk averse – nor could he be in Iraq. 'We like risk,' he says, 'it's good for our business.' However, 'there is a limit [at which] it becomes impossible [for us] to function. I'm not here to resolve the conflict, or eradicate the insurgency. I'm here to protect people.'

Blackwater would no doubt ask: who protects those who need to operate beyond his risk limits? In Iraq, there are many exceedingly risky situations that create a need for protection. In trying to meet this need, contractors become an obvious target. Westropp concedes that it is 'partially true' that his operation benefits from the easier targets presented by deliberately high-profile companies like Blackwater.

Blackwater both accepts riskier assignments and takes this more aggressive stance with plenty of arms, armour and visibility. (Ironically, and sadly, according to a lawsuit lodged against the company by the families of the four dead Fallujah contractors, they were not armed and protected to Blackwater policy standards when they were ambushed.) As a result 26 of its employees had died in Iraq up to the time of writing. This appears to be a higher mortality rate than its competitors – Control Risks has lost only two employees – although the numbers are difficult to compare and unreliable.

The men on the ground

Even with the best intelligence, tactics and equipment, in an environment as hazardous as Iraq, in the notorious words of former, US Secretary of Defense Donald Rumsfeld, 'stuff' will still happen. Indeed, during the interview with Westropp a call came through: one of his convoys had been hit by a roadside bomb. Fortunately no one was killed.

The last strand of both *planning* and *doing* is making sure that if an attack occurs, the men on the ground have both the skills and discipline to execute the chosen tactics. Westropp emphasizes that 'we very carefully screen and train our employees. Before taking someone on we conduct detailed background checks and psychometric tests. In Iraq, every week our teams practise a range of contingencies, such as ambush and cross-loading [transferring people between vehicles].' Blackwater was founded by former US Navy SEALS (naval special forces), and while its growth has forced it to cast its net wider, and even train its own staff from scratch, it retains a keen interest in recruiting former special forces operatives. Consistent with his strategy of blending in, the unnamed CEO prefers staff with paramilitary and covert action backgrounds rather than special forces.

Finally, there is a last line of defence for westerners in Iraq: the Coalition military. If a firm's tactical response, be it escape or counterattack, fails, it can call on the military for assistance, such as air support. Importantly, this only works reliably if the firm has notified the military of the mission and received clearance. Blackwater's mission into Fallujah had not been discussed with the local military commanders.

THE MILITARY

Military personnel managing terrorism risk use the same underlying process of intelligence-led deployment of highly skilled and disciplined personnel as civilian agencies, but with a wider remit and a higher risk appetite. The military is the only organization covered in this book that explicitly tolerates casualties. A former officer in the UK Special Forces (UKSF), who spoke on condition of anonymity, observes that '[the armed forces] are self-selected: we want to take risk, we want to fight. I never heard of any [SF soldier] refusing a mission.' In most cases, the limit on their operations is the risk appetite of their political masters. The risk appetite of politicians is 'far lower than [that of] the armed forces. It's extremely unlikely that we would get the go-ahead for an operation that was beyond our risk appetite.'

Another key difference is that in addition to protecting terrorist targets, the military also conducts proactive anti-terrorist operations. For example in September 2005 two UKSF personnel were detained by police in southern Iraq and handed over to local militia. Most sources report that they were part of an operation to disrupt terrorist supply lines from Iran. In keeping with the higher risk appetite of the military, the men were freed after the army sent armoured vehicles crashing through the wall of the compound where they were being held. The former UKSF officer notes approvingly that this was 'high risk, gutsy… it's good to see that officers in the British Army still feel able to make those kind of calls'.

Intelligence – on the location of the men and their probable fate – supported this 'call'. In real time, the commanding officer decided to send in the cavalry (literally). As for civilians, such intelligence plays a central role in the *plan/do* cycle. The UKSF officer notes that every operation he was involved in – in the Balkans, in Northern Ireland, in Afghanistan and elsewhere – was underwritten by intelligence.

Officers develop detailed mission plans based on the available intelligence. The plans face intense questioning to test and re-test the thought process, and they continue to evolve up to the last minute. He explains that 'ultimately we delegate both the planning and the final go/no-go to the team leader. They're the one with the best information.' Given this approach, 'the culture of the organization needs to be supportive of saying no' and cancelling an operation.

A former UK commando, currently working with a security firm in Iraq, adds:

You plan to the minutest detail before going in… [to prevent the] four main things [that] can go wrong: you're compromised [attacked before reaching the objective], your equipment fails, someone gets injured, or the weather turns bad. There are occasions when it turns into a [unspeakable act], of course.

In that case, the men on the ground have to sort it out as best they can. They are best able to do this if they are highly skilled and highly trained. Both men emphasize the role of training and selection in the successful execution of operations. The former UKSF officer adds that 'training enables decentralization. If skilled individuals get to problems early and [have the latitude to] sort them out, then the situation stays under control.' This illustrates another recurring theme of this book: that highly trained responders can contain events before they compound and escalate.

UKSF selection and training

Over a toasted ham and cheese sandwich, helpfully colour-coded 'yellow – moderate levels of fat and salt' on the Officers' Mess menu, a serving Lieutenant Colonel in UKSF explains in more detail how the Special Air Service (SAS) regiment selects and trains its personnel.

> Selection takes place twice a year over 24 weeks. The application process [is]... as open as possible. It's the only course in the UK military that commanding officers can't refuse permission for. Everyone who wants to have a go, gets a go. The aim is to select men for service while training them up to SF standards. If they pass they are ready to go on a mission and – at the very least – not be a burden.
>
> We want hard men, men who go on when they're exhausted. [For example] in the fourth week of Selection, [the candidates] must complete a series of six increasingly difficult hill marches carrying a certain load within a certain time... the time limit obviously implies a certain average speed, but [that's] not the point. The point is that if at any point you can run, you must.

Candidates must complete the sixth and final hill march of 64 kilometres carrying a fully-loaded pack in 20 hours.

> The officers' leadership skills and intelligence – their creativity, innovation and confidence – are [also] tested. Being an officer in SF is a difficult job... all the men are natural leaders, officers have to earn the right to command... an officer who relied on rank alone would fail. Each day for a week they will be given a series of operational problems to solve – such as 'how would you have neutralized the Argentine air threat over Port Stanley?' They have three hours to prepare, then they have to make a presentation to a mixed audience of SF personnel, from NCOs [non-commissioned officers] to the Brigadier. They face intense questioning. They will be busy from 0500 to 0100 every day... if they choose to sleep. The idea is to see how they cope with increasingly difficult problems under increasing levels of stress and sleep deprivation.

Following these tests, the candidates then undertake four weeks of jungle training in Asia, then return to the United Kingdom.

> The last test is Combat Survival. It's all very World War Two. They're searched, taken out at night in a lorry, then given a hand-

drawn map (with some deliberate mistakes and omissions), a compass, and a grid reference, and told to be at the rendezvous by a certain time. A hunter force is in pursuit. After five days of this, they are subjected to 36 hours of detention with periods of interrogation. Their instructions are to say nothing at all beyond the six Geneva requirements of name, rank, number, date of birth, blood type and religion.

We're most interested in personal characteristics and qualities than can't be taught, such as determination, robustness and integrity. Selection is a means to identify these qualities. The process is intentionally arduous. The failure rate is high, 85 to 90 per cent.

Subsequent training is continuous. [It] depends on individual needs and programmed overseas exercises. We have about 150 courses available internally, some of them highly specialized. We have highly standardized procedures, such as counter-ambush, that we train to such a degree that reactions are automatic. There is no separation between doctrine, operations and training. Mission planning assumes a minimum level of accomplishment. Anything less compromises our risk appetite.

The combination of highly selective entry and rigorous training creates a virtuous circle: a strong skill base permits difficult missions, which in turn allows the accumulation of expertise; this accumulation of expertise allows better training, and yet more difficult missions. As elsewhere, as you practise in extreme environments, you get better at coping with the surprises they throw up.

Events do not always conform to the plan. There is an apt military aphorism, attributed to Prussian Field Marshal von Moltke, that 'no plan survives contact with the enemy'. According to the book and film *Black Hawk Down*, mentioned in the Preface, highly selective and highly trained US Special Forces units rehearsed intensively prior to deploying in Mogadishu. They practised everything that ended up happening, including the downing of a Black Hawk helicopter. However, when a second Black Hawk went down, they had to commit all their ground forces to its recovery. Having no forces in reserve, they then had to ask for help from the United Nations (UN) forces to relieve their troops at the crash sites. It appears that the one contingency they hadn't anticipated was having to ask for help. For example, they had not informed the UN of their plans, and they had no interpreters. Assembling support from the UN took a long time, and the US soldiers ended up in a bloody all-night battle. The United States subsequently withdrew from Somalia.

The incident ends up underlining the difference in risk appetite between the military and their civilian overseers. Participants in the battle are quoted as saying that 'it is astonishing that the calculus of success is a single casualty. Every [man] there will tell you it was a victory.' They do not understand why the United States withdrew.

RISK SEEKING

The fact that the military tolerate casualties does not mean that they do not *think* about risk. They are not suicidal. Rather, it simply means that they are risk-seeking. They want to take risk, but intelligently. Equally, it does not mean that they do not *plan* to manage the risks they take. One of the striking things about talking to serving and former military personnel is that it takes them some time to understand what you mean when you talk about risk management. For them, risk management is not a separate function that tells them what they can and cannot do, it's one of their core competences. From their point of view, risk management is inherent in and inseparable from their daily activities. If it weren't, in a place like Iraq they'd quickly end up dead. Anyone who doesn't manage their risk to a high standard is perceived as a liability and ostracized.

The former UKSF officer relates how on a mission:

> We were in the back of the Land Rover, expecting contact [a fight] any minute. Everyone was quiet, going through the plan in their heads, controlling their fear – except for one bloke at the back, who was mouthing off. He hadn't been in a fight before and I guess this was his way of compensating. I decided that the first thing I would do when we got out of the Land Rover was hit him in the head with my rifle butt. He was too dangerous; I couldn't accept the risk that he posed to the operation.

Civilian risk managers in Iraq follow the same process of *planning* and *doing*, just anchored at a lower level of risk. Like the military, the keys to managing their risks are twofold. First, if intelligence indicates that the threat is over their risk appetite level, they don't leave base. Second, if something happens, they ensure that their staff are able to execute their chosen tactics effectively. These principles are similar to those used by risk managers in extreme aid environments and the mountains (see Chapters 4 and 5).

The same keys apply in principle to *planning* and *doing* terrorism risk management in the London Underground and other civilian targets. If intelligence indicates an imminent attack, close the target down; if an attack occurs, ensure that your search and rescue teams execute the recovery plan quickly and effectively. While the Underground has yet to be pre-emptively shut down, Heathrow airport and many individual stations have been.

However, uncertainty is greater in a country at peace than in Iraq. This affects two aspects of risk management: target hardening and intelligence gathering. Terrorism in Iraq is so widespread that every government, military and corporate installation is a terrorist target and needs fortification. In peaceful countries there are many possible targets but few terrorists. Beyond the most obvious targets such as stores of uranium or plutonium, major transport hubs and the seat of government, choosing which targets to harden is subject to diminishing returns. Even as one target is hardened, others become more attractive by displacement. In practice it is not feasible to harden every potential target. In a sense risk management in Iraq is simpler since the threats are so manifest. Everything is a target and will almost certainly be targeted at some point. In London everything might be a target but most likely nothing will ever happen.

Without the clarity supplied by an extreme environment, it is difficult for intelligence information to be robust enough to justify closing down such large and economically important systems as the London Underground. The UK government acknowledges this in its public counter-terrorism strategy documents, saying:

> It is rare that specific threat information is available and can be relied upon. More often, judgements about the threat will be based on a wide range of information, which is often fragmentary, including the level and nature of current terrorist activity, comparison with events in other countries and previous attacks. Intelligence is only ever likely to reveal part of the picture.

That said, directing more resources at intelligence and response is probably more worthwhile than hardening targets, even if the latter is more televisual. Gordon Woo, a terrorism risk expert at RMS, a catastrophe risk modelling firm (see box), postulates a tipping point in intelligence. Below a certain level of activity, no pattern is evident. Above this point, 'a far more obvious signature may become apparent... the most ambitious plans are thus liable to be thwarted... too many terrorists spoil the plot'.

Risk appetite in peacetime is also less clear-cut. In the same document the UK government states:

> It is not possible to eliminate completely the threat of terrorist attacks in this country... the government can never guarantee that attacks will not

happen in the future, but its security effort is dedicated to reducing the risk as much as possible.

Such imprecision is inevitable since in peacetime terrorism risk appetite is expressed collectively rather than individually. Risk appetite becomes implicit rather than explicit. There is not the sense of imminent personal threat experienced in Iraq. As for epidemics, a society expresses its collective risk appetite through its tolerance of expenditure and inconvenience. The RAND institute, a think tank based in San Francisco with strong links to the US government, is actively researching societal risk appetite. RAND notes in a 2006 paper that:

> Establishing tolerable levels of risk is one of the most contentious and important risk management decisions. With every regulatory or funding decision for a risk management program, society decides whether or not a risk is tolerable. If risks are deemed too large, regulations are established and resources allocated. If risks are tolerated, activities remain unregulated and resources are often directed elsewhere.

To try to influence collective risk perception, and hence both behaviour and appetite for expenditure and restrictions, both the US and UK governments have started publishing their official, intelligence-based 'threat level'.

GOVERNMENT RESPONSE

Beyond publishing threat levels, the UK and US governments are responding to these uncertainties in more fundamental ways. They are improving their key risk management activities – intelligence gathering and emergency response – in three ways: increasing police and intelligence service power, supporting quantitative risk research, and improving inter-agency emergency cooperation. In addition, they are engaged in a deeply controversial effort to reduce the frequency of terrorism by intervening in 'terrorist safe havens'.

Since 11 September 2001, many governments have widened their powers to spy on, detain and prosecute suspected terrorists and their supporters. This increases intelligence gathered, and potentially prevents suspects from participating in or supporting attacks. For example, the current US administration created the Guantanamo Bay detention centre so that it could detain and interrogate suspected terrorists indefinitely, and has interpreted the law regarding communications interception (such as phone tapping) broadly so that it could extend surveillance efforts. Among other measures, the UK government has doubled the length of time police can detain a terrorist suspect to 28 days and made it illegal 'directly or indirectly to encourage the commission, preparation or instigation of acts of terrorism or to disseminate terrorist publications'. These measures, some of which were not disclosed at the time, are now extremely controversial. If they do not lead to numerous convictions in the next year or two, public support for their continuation will erode.

In parallel, governments have supported and encouraged research into modelling efforts to try to better understand and quantify the risk (see box). In addition, governments have tried to enhance emergency response capabilities. The US Federal government centralized all its emergency response functions in the Department of Homeland Security (DHS) (albeit with questionable results). Less controversially, it also adopted California's Standard Emergency Management System (SEMS, see Chapter 9) as a nationwide emergency response standard. In the UK, the 2004 Civil Contingency Act (CCA) provided a common framework and structure for emergency response and planning work across agencies. It too appears heavily influenced by SEMS.

Modelling 'macroterrorism'

How do you quantify the risk of terrorist attacks? Following 11 September 2001, the RAND Institute and the catastrophe risk modelling firm RMS (see also Chapters 8 on floods and 9 on earthquakes) worked for the US DHS to estimate US 'macroterrorism' risk – the frequency and severity of terrorist events that cause over 100 deaths or 500 casualties.

Uniquely in this book, their models combine simulation and expert judgement on an equal footing. The models use simulation where the data are rich, such as weather patterns (for fallout dispersal), explosive effects and the physical strength and layout of a city's buildings (for damage assessment, blast propagation and shielding). In tandem, they use regular expert assessments of more subjective elements such as terrorist target selection, attack patterns and capabilities (suicide bombings, surface-to-air missiles, CBRN, etc). The expert assessment process includes the application of game theory, so that the responses of the terrorists evolve with the risk management measures employed. For example, as government targets are hardened, civilian targets are substituted. The models allow users to select any location or 'high-risk target' and predict the impact of any one of 32 'attack modes'. Among other findings, it concludes that New York is only US city that receives the highest risk rating. AIR, another catastrophe risk modelling firm, has also launched a terrorism loss model with similar characteristics.

RMS claims that the absence of macro-terrorist attacks in 2003 and 2004 as a result of ongoing disruption of al-Qaeda's network was in line with its predictions. It remains to be seen how well these models' predictions prove out in the long term, especially given the inherent rarity of such 'macroterrorism' attacks.

The response to the 7 July 2005 bombings in London, while not perfect, was a good example of inter-agency cooperation as mandated by the CCA, according to those involved. As noted above, Ogden felt that 'our interaction with other agencies was spot on, it was the slickest rescue operation I'd ever seen'. His boss Nick Collins, the duty assistant commissioner on the day and the LFB's head of strategic risk management, notes that 'We plan for much worse events than 7/7. That was just like training.'

The London Regional Resilience Forum felt that 'the multi-agency response to the 7 July bombings was very successful', noting, for example, the evacuation of the entire London transport system without incident, the provision of 1,200 hospital beds within three hours, and the smooth functioning of the incident management structure. The Forum criticized overdependence on mobile phones and the arrangements for looking after the injured and their families.

INTERVENTION UPSTREAM

Finally, and most controversially, some governments aim to directly reduce the frequency of terrorist attacks by addressing the causes of terrorism. Most risk managers do not have the ability to change the system 'upstream' in this way. No one can change the weather or the movements of tectonic plates; risk managers outside China can only marginally influence risky poultry farming practices inside China. In contrast, the US government counter-terrorism strategy states that:

> In the short run, the fight [against terrorism] involves the application of all instruments of national power and influence to kill or capture the terrorists; deny them safe haven and control of any nation; prevent them from gaining access to WMD; render potential terrorist targets less attractive

by strengthening security; and cut off their sources of funding and other resources they need to operate and survive.

Clearly, killing terrorists should reduce terrorism. In addition, if terrorists operate from territorial or financial safe havens, then eliminating these havens should reduce their operational effectiveness. Denying al-Qaeda safe haven in Afghanistan and killing or capturing many of its leaders appear to have reduced its ability to conduct terrorist operations. However, it is questionable whether the invasion of Iraq will further reduce terrorism, since the causality appears to be backwards. There were no terrorists threatening Western countries from Iraq before the invasion. Rather, the invasion itself was the primary cause of the wave of terrorism in Iraq and a powerful stimulus to it elsewhere, as US and UK intelligence and diplomatic services have argued since 2003.

In addition, identifying terrorists before they act is hard. The academic consensus is that there is no way to determine whether a given individual will become a terrorist or not, or why certain groups adopt terrorist tactics and others do not. The same US counterterrorism document states that: 'In the long run, winning the War on Terror means winning the battle of ideas. Ideas can transform the embittered and disillusioned either into murderers willing to kill innocents, or into free peoples living harmoniously in a diverse society.' This can also work in reverse. Arresting and detaining thousands of people is unlikely to identify many terrorists and very unlikely to win the 'battle of ideas'.

For risk managers, the point is that there are sometimes great uncertainties in the upstream causes of risk, and the costs of attempting to manage these risks can be greater than the benefits. Before starting on such a course of action, these costs and benefits need to be carefully analysed and understood. Just as when managing the risk of wildfires or epidemics, the simplest answer isn't always the best way of managing risk in the long term.

APPLICATION TO BUSINESS

The most obvious application of these concepts to business is in managing terrorism risk. As in other areas, businesses need to assess their terrorism risk against their corporate risk appetite. If the risk is above the risk appetite (this is unlikely for the majority of firms), the firm has three options. First, if the excess risk is result of location in or near a likely terrorist target, such as the World Trade Center in New York, activities can be relocated. The brokerage firm Morgan Stanley employed over

3,000 people in the World Trade Center in 2001. According to a profile in the *New Yorker*, the late John Rescorla, a decorated Vietnam veteran and the company's head of security, had 'concluded that the company should leave the World Trade Center and build quarters in New Jersey, preferably a three- or four-storey complex spread over a large area'. By 11 September 2001 the firm had already made this decision but was waiting for its lease to expire.

Second, if relocation is not an option for business reasons, or the firm itself is a target for symbolic or political reasons, the firm must reduce vulnerability to terrorism. This requires a detailed assessment of the firm's sources of vulnerability and the implementation of extensive changes to facilities and procedures to remedy them. The changes tend to cover the waterfront, from installing back-up utility supplies to improving perimeter fencing, to imposing more stringent pre-employment screening.

Third, firms need to recognize that an attack may occur, and prepare. At one level this means ensuring that staff are familiar with emergency procedures. At another it means having sufficiently skilled personnel charged with emergency response, just as in Iraq. Such policies also reduce risk from other events such as fires and earthquakes. As part of Rescorla's plan, Morgan Stanley had instituted a highly structured evacuation drill:

> At a command from [Rescorla], which would come over the intercom system, all employees were instructed to move to the emergency staircases. Starting with the top floor, they were to prepare to march downstairs in twos, so that someone would be alongside to help if anyone stumbled. As the last pair from one floor reached the floor below, employees from that floor would fall in behind them. The drill was practiced twice a year.

Its successful execution on 9/11 saved all but six employees. One of the six was Rescorla, who died as he searched the offices for stragglers.

A more general application of the concepts of this chapter is in the management of extremely risky businesses. There are many high-risk segments in financial services, from lending to consumers with poor credit records and limited incomes to speculating on commodities futures. Businesses that plan to survive the next downturn in these segments can learn from the practices in this chapter.

First, if the data indicates that a deal is too risky, don't leave base – just don't go there. A good example of this is the way in which investment banks manage the timing of capital markets transactions such as initial public offerings (IPOs) or bond issues. If the conditions are not favourable, they postpone them. For example, between January and September 2006

33 companies had postponed their IPOs because of market conditions, according to Dealogic. While it is embarrassing for all concerned to postpone such a transaction, embarrassment beats failure.

Second, if there really is no choice but to undertake a risky transaction – say an important customer insists you underwrite a transaction for a related firm – 'harden the target' by imposing conditions that enable you to survive if things turn out badly. For a loan, these conditions might include a formal guarantee, a pledge of collateral, or clauses in the loan agreement that allow increasing control over the transaction. For a trade, they might be contractual conditions such as the initial margin amount (the amount a counterparty has to post in collateral prior to trading), or internal conditions such as the size of the required hedge or a limit on the maximum permitted loss (the 'stop-loss'). The processes to enforce these conditions under stress are as important as the conditions themselves.

Third, keep some experienced, highly skilled people on staff to perform the 'rescue mission' if stuff ends up happening. In a lending operation, they would be 'work-out' specialists, debt collectors; in a trading environment, they would be traders in distressed securities. While they are expensive and often cranky individuals, and difficult both to justify and to manage in the good times, in the bad times such experts pay back the investment through their hard-won expertise in negotiation, liquidation procedures and corporate restructurings.

At the highest level of abstraction, the management of terrorism risk illustrates clearly that risk cannot be eliminated. No matter how hard you try, some level of risk will always persist. Basing any risk management strategy on the premise that it will be able to 'solve' the risk is delusional.

In the next chapter we analyse a closely related environment, managing the risk of aid workers in conflict and near-conflict areas.

4

Extreme humanitarian aid

Interviewees

David Nott	Consultant general surgeon at the Chelsea and West-minster hospital, London, UK; serial Médecins sans Frontières (MSF) volunteer
Gareth Owen	Head of logistics and security, Save The Children, UK
Luke Atkinson	Demining programme manager, Norwegian People's Aid (NPA), Sri Lanka
Bruno Lab	Head of operations, MSF Switzerland
Geir Bjorsvik	Director of research, NPA, Norway

Humanitarian aid seeks to save lives and alleviate suffering. Extreme humanitarian aid attempts this in life or death situations, such as natural disasters, infectious disease outbreaks or violent conflicts. Chapters 8 and 9 cover managing the risk of two types of natural disaster, flooding and earthquakes. Chapter 1 covers the risk management of infectious disease outbreaks. This chapter focuses on managing the risk to aid workers operating in active violent conflicts and their immediate aftermath.

David Nott, a consultant general surgeon at the Chelsea and Westminster hospital in London and serial Médecins sans Frontières (MSF) volunteer, shares an MSF in-joke. 'There's a five-stage progression in a conflict. First the government leaves town; then any civilians who can, do the same; then the ICRC [International Committee of the Red Cross] evacuates; then the rebels enter the town; and then MSF arrives.'

At its foundation in 1971, MSF stated its objective 'to throw down the barriers, the frontiers... between those who whose vocation is caring and healing and the victims of human barbarism'. One way to operate in an extreme aid environment is to seek out active conflicts like MSF. Another is to work in an unstable post-conflict or near-conflict situation and not exit before 'the rebels enter town'. A third is to undertake intrinsically hazardous projects such as clearing mines and other explosive remnants of war (ERW). We shall examine risk management in each of these three types of extreme aid in turn.

In 1994 Nott volunteered for a surgical mission in Sarajevo, Bosnia (then part of Yugoslavia). It was an extreme environment for sure, an active conflict:

> After we touched down, the plane turned round [unloaded, reloaded and took off again] in just 14 minutes to make sure it wouldn't get hit on the runway. We were taken by armoured personnel carrier to town. The hospital where we were based had so many holes it looked like it was made of Swiss cheese. We operated underground, wearing helmets and flak jackets the whole time, while above ground about 2,000 shells a day were landing.
>
> We stayed underground almost the entire time. Once we went up to the ground floor [of the hospital] to have a look around. Within a minute or two a sniper put two bullets into the wall over our heads, politely letting us know that this was a bad idea. We only left the basement one other time.

That one other time was almost one too many:

> We were going mad being cooped up all the time, so we went out one day to have a beer after surgery. The restaurant was underground, which was normal, but full of very odd-looking characters. We'd just sat down when a shoot-out began, bullets everywhere, just like a Wild West saloon. We dropped to the floor and pulled our table over us, waited until the shooting stopped, then ran for it. I have no idea what it was about and I wasn't going to stick around to find out.

Active conflicts are extreme environments, even when you're off-duty.

Gareth Owen, now head of logistics and security for aid organization Save The Children (STC), was a novice aid worker in Malange, Angola, in 1993. His experience there illustrates a second type of extreme aid environment, when conflict overtakes a mission:

> The 400,000 people living [in Malange] were in danger of starvation. We were airlifted in... to set up a feeding programme for 16,000 children under five and 2,000 high-risk adults. I'd had no formal briefing before I arrived beyond a 'dangerous but OK' assessment from a professional security advisor. I learnt the rest as I went along, the difference between the sound of an incoming and an outgoing shell, that kind of thing.

> After we'd dealt with the original danger, food shortage, a new one
> emerged – anarchy. [As the situation deteriorated] we had to have armed
> guards to protect the food, otherwise it would have been stolen. We had to
> use live rounds to keep people away from the food.

After the anarchy came conflict:

> The town was physically blockaded [by rebels] and subject to intermittent
> skirmishes. Then the rebels broke the air bridge and we were completely
> cut off. We became a bargaining chip in the negotiations. We begged a
> mercy flight; then we had to insist that they evacuate non-local Angolans
> too… [as] we were afraid of what might happen to them… I remember
> shouting 'If they're staying, so am I.' Then one of my staff tried to stay
> behind and I had to physically drag him onto the plane.

What started as a difficult post-conflict environment reverted to an active
conflict and became extreme.

Mine clearance is an example of a third type of extreme aid environment: this is concerned with the post-conflict removal of mines and
other explosive remnants of war. According to the Geneva International
Centre for Humanitarian Demining (GICHD), in 1944–45 an unfortunate
German prisoner-of-war mine clearance brigade operating in the Nether-
lands recorded 543 casualties, including 162 dead, out of 3,244 men.
After the first Gulf War in 1991, the Kuwaitis organized a large-scale
mine clearance. According to *Landmine Monitor*, a publication of the
International Campaign to Ban Landmines, 'it involved 4,000 expatriate
deminers, eighty-four of whom were killed during the operation'. Luke
Atkinson, a demining programme manager for Norwegian People's
Aid (NPA), observes that 'the casualties in Kuwait were unacceptable.
The clearance teams were all internationals, their contracts applied
commercial pressures [to rush the job], and IMAS [International Mine
Action Standards] were not applied.' Even without an active conflict,
clearing mines is an extremely risky activity.

NO ACCIDENT

All three types of extreme environment – indeed, all aid work – involve
significant risks to aid workers. Unexpectedly, with the possible excep-
tion of Iraq, the largest risks to aid workers are from infectious diseases
and road accidents. For example, only half the fatalities suffered by NPA
since its foundation have been caused by land mines. Aid workers accept
these baseline risks, in line with their own personal risk appetites, as part

of the job. Risk seekers volunteer for Afghanistan; risk-averse individuals, Thailand. Bruno Lab, head of operations for MSF Switzerland, expresses this as 'zero risk is not part of the esprit of MSF'. Certainly MSF volunteers are not in it for the money. Nott notes dryly that 'unlike [other organizations] at MSF you get expenses only, not the market rate for your skills'.

Aid organization *thinking* about risk distinguishes between accidents and health risks, professional risks such as explosions, and deliberate actions such as kidnapping, rape and murder. Aid workers can tolerate and mitigate accidents, health risks and professional risks. Deliberate harm to aid workers is unacceptable, and defines the limit of aid agency risk tolerance. The critical part of *thinking* about risk is then assessing the likelihood of such deliberate harm.

Aid agencies make these assessments increasingly carefully, says Owen:

> Risk assessment used to consist of one or two old dogs who would go round [before the mission] and sniff the air... it was a bit generic, 'don't drive at night', that kind of thing. Humanitarian agencies needed to get better at risk management – we're supposed to be there to help, not [to] get into trouble. This has improved somewhat since a group of agencies got together in 2000 and created a template for risk assessment.

In addition, he observes that 'the tolerance for body-count has changed. This has been driven in large part by the insurance companies, which since 11 September 2001 have become more reluctant to insure aid workers.' As a result 'there has also been significant professionalization, and outsourcing of security to private military contractors'.

One factor behind this professionalization is the perception that risks to aid workers have increased since the start of 'the global war on terror' (the statistics are unclear). Owen says that in his experience 'there has been a breakdown in the respect accorded to humanitarian missions... agencies are now perceived as part of the problem... this has become a very dangerous trade'.

If the possibility of deliberate harm to aid workers is high, aid agencies investigate the possibility of negotiating a security guarantee from local powers. If no guarantee seems possible, aid agencies kill the mission before it starts. This may be because the environment is simply too hazardous for anyone except the military. For example, parts of Iraq are completely off-limits to all non-military westerners. It may also happen at the border between crisis and normality, where there is neither an immediate crisis nor a central authority. In this situation, local militias are able to fill the vacuum without providing any stability, as in Somalia. In these cases, humanitarian aid may prove impossible to deliver. Conversely, extreme aid organizations can also decide that the risks are not high enough. For example, MSF Switzerland has exited EU-member-to-be Bulgaria.

If a guarantee is thought possible, the first stage of mission *planning* is then, according to MSF, to 'establish transparent relationships with local authorities and communities based on unambiguous humanitarian identity'. This means identifying and contacting all powerful local parties – some of whom may be quite unsavoury, such as drug-running Afghan warlords – and negotiating a promise not to intervene, on the basis that the aid work is purely humanitarian and not aligned with any particular faction or agenda.

Another risk inherent in extreme aid activities is psychological. Nott's cheerful tone disappears when he talks of his most recent experience, with MSF in Darfur, Sudan in 2004:

> My previous assignments had been in conflict zones, so we were basically dealing with combat casualties. In Darfur, it was mostly obstetrics. There was no food, no water, extreme heat and constant danger. Maternal mortality was one in eight. We lived in a compound in the middle of this sea of refugees. We only left to go to the surgery. Once a week we would trawl through the camps and decide who to try to save. We had one surgeon trying to cover 2.2 million refugees. It was extremely distressing, the most difficult thing I've done in my life.

It seems that when risks are not shared by both aid workers and aid recipients, a psychological burden builds up on the former. While this is a recognized risk, few aid organizations appear to manage it proactively.

LOGISTICS

Alongside these negotiations with local actors, extreme aid organizations work up evacuation plans. The objective is to ensure that if conditions change – 'the rebels arrive' or a non-intervention agreement breaks down – aid workers can be evacuated rapidly and discreetly. Before any aid workers are deployed in a country, security personnel identify and assess escape routes and develop evacuation procedures.

Once an aid agency has negotiated a non-intervention agreement with locals and established an evacuation plan, the final stage of planning is logistical. The aid organization needs to organize transportation, accommodation and resupply, potentially through hostile terrain. In general, as a point of principle, extreme aid providers try not to rely on anyone else

– Lab states that 'MSF does not call on other actors, period.' This creates a formidable logistical challenge. For example, transporting food to aid workers through a famine-ravaged country without government or UN support is very high risk. Equally, almost all transactions are in cash, so aid workers often carry large amounts of cash, making them an even more tempting target.

While aid organizations sometimes protect supplies with armed guards, they do not in general use them to protect the mission itself. Owen notes that '[armed guards] usually don't work. In Somalia we had armed guards, but when our workers were ambushed by hostage takers, our guards ended up running out of ammunition.' MSF has had similar experiences, and consequently its policy is to employ unarmed guards. The bad guys have more guns and fewer qualms about using them.

When the aid workers are in place, they are exposed to the hazards of the working environment. This residual risk is accepted and managed actively as part of the process of *doing*. Communicating these risks, and deciding how to mitigate them, is central to the risk management function in aid organizations. Prior to arrival, aid workers receive pre-mission briefings covering objectives, environment and risks. In some cases they undergo 'hostile environment training', where they role-play car accidents, getting lost in minefields and being kidnapped. In country, aid workers receive ongoing assessments, briefings and training.

Sensitizing aid workers to the risk is complicated by the fact that, according to Owen, 'often the least experienced personnel are in the riskiest environments... Kandahar in 2003 was full of first-timers.' Presumably the old-timers knew the underlying level of risk and declined the proposition.

Most aid agencies 'reduce visibility as far as possible', according to Lab. This is achieved by providing aid workers with secure accommodation, transportation and workplaces – and forbidding them to leave. To enforce this policy, aid organizations provide carrots and sticks. Security briefings provide carrots – it's in your own interest to follow the rules. Codes of conduct and contracts that spell out rights, responsibilities, disciplinary procedures and insurance coverage provide sticks – follow the rules or else. Workers who do not are weeded out or end up dead. 'Mavericks don't last', says Owen.

Even draconian rules do not always work. Lab admits that 'we cannot easily order [MSF volunteers] around... they always have the choice'. Despite his Wild West experience in Bosnia, a couple of years later when working for the ICRC in Kandahar, Afghanistan, Nott defied policy again and took a trip to the Khyber pass (albeit with a driver and guards this time).

In high-risk countries, the risk assessment process is continuous. For example, STC requires operations in high-risk countries to provide an updated risk assessment, security guidelines and training every six months, or after every incident, whichever is sooner. The local MSF logistics and security manager categorizes the security status of the operation as green, yellow, red or black. Black means imminent evacuation. This call is delegated to the local manager.

In addition, local logistics teams ensure that vehicles are fully serviced and full of fuel, and walkie-talkies fully charged. Team members keep track of each other through contact cascades. Rehearsals of evacuation are rare, partly since the procedures are simple ('drop everything and get in the truck') and partly because it would difficult to gain the trust of the local community if it were perceived that the aid workers always had one foot out of the door.

MSF LEAVES AFGHANISTAN

MSF's experience in Afghanistan illustrates both what happens when a local security guarantee breaks down and the increasing risk to aid work since 2001. After 24 years of continuous operations in Afghanistan, in 2004 MSF withdrew following the assassination of five of its staff. Lab says sadly 'in the end it was a pretty easy decision: it was assassination, cold-blooded murder. Everyone knew who did it, that it would go unpunished, that MSF was still a target, and [that] it would happen again.' MSF terminated the mission and repatriated its volunteers.

While the decision may have been easy from a logical point of view, this was a difficult decision for MSF after working for such a long time in Afghanistan. Lab for one is clearly personally upset. 'Before 2001 [during the civil war], we worked side by side with the Mujahadeen [Afghan resistance fighters]. We'd never even used armed guards. Even under the Taleban there was no systematic hostility.' After the invasion in 2001, according to a UN-sponsored publication (Stoddard and Harmer, 2005: see Resources), 'US military forces travelled in unmarked vehicles in civilian clothes, carried concealed weapons, and identified themselves as humanitarians.' As a result, says Lab bitterly, 'all foreigners were suspected of taking part in a grand project: the Americanization of Afghanistan. We were either with them or against them, and they decided we were against them. It seems that [President Bush's view that "you're either with us or against us"] cuts both ways.'

The chilling thing about this situation is that if a local non-intervention agreement breaks down, you already know what will happen, where it will happen, and probably when it will happen and by whom. For the risk manager, the key issue is to keep linking *doing* back to *thinking*, and comparing the current level of risk with the original risk appetite.

DEMINING

In post-conflict demining missions, where the primary activity is intrinsically hazardous as well as the location, there is additional risk. This risk has two elements: the risk of injury to the mine clearer and the residual risk after the activity to the users of the cleared minefield. For example, mines may blow up as they are cleared, injuring the mine clearer; or, if undiscovered, they may blow up later and injure a local farmer.

Managing the risk to mine clearers is the more straightforward of the two. Deminers are in control of their actions and the site, and their incentives are very clear. Because they operate in an intrinsically hazardous environment, if they don't do the job properly and take appropriate precautions, they will most certainly be badly hurt or killed. If they do manage their risk, they can't be completely safe, but they can reduce the risk to sustainable levels.

For example, Atkinson, a former paratrooper with a degree in anthropology and religious studies, describes his recent experience in Sri Lanka:

> The programme is based in the principal town in the LTTE [Tamil Tiger-controlled zone], Kilinochchi. There were many refugees returning [but] it wasn't safe. A Tamil organization had put together a team of locals. They did a lot of good work but lots of people were getting blown up. They denied it, but you could see the blast marks on their faces.
>
> Many of the deminers had been in combat... [but] walking through a minefield is not like running at machine guns... no heroic sacrifices are required... if people are getting hurt, that means they're doing it wrong.

On at least one occasion, a deminer put a mine in his pocket only to sit on it later:

> You need to make a system and stick to it, otherwise you don't know what you've done. There was no control of the minefield. They couldn't tell us if they'd cleared a field... so we're now reclearing the areas that they'd attempted. They typically got about 80 per cent [of the mines].

There were other safety issues too. For example, there were many snakes, but no access to snake anti-venom or a doctor. However, 'since the programme started, we've trained 600 people, and they've cleared 30,000 mines with no accidents'.

Geir Bjorsvik, Atkinson's colleague and the director of research at NPA, agrees that 'if you follow procedures, there is very limited risk [in demining]'. He is using a high standard, though. For example, he observes that a risk appetite of one in 10,000, used elsewhere as a proxy for 'as low as reasonably practicable', is too high for mine clearance. A square kilometre is 1,000 metres per side, with a total area of 1 million square metres. If only one in every 10,000 square metres has an undiscovered mine, that means that each square kilometre contains 100 mines. This is much too high for, say, a cultivated field, where the farmer will walk every square metre repeatedly.

Demining procedures

Deminers manage their personal risk by applying a rigorous and well-documented system. First, they consult the local population to identify and characterize the field to clear. They then survey the field's terrain, history and ERW load. Team leaders feed the results from the survey into a planning process. The plan generates detailed resource requirements in line with the complexity and risk of the clearance. For example, clearing anti-tank mines laid according to standard army practices on a road far from the front lines will require a different quantity and type of resource than clearing anti-personnel mines laid randomly by paramilitaries in a field on the front line. The plans will include an explicit statement of risk appetite, stating as an objective that a certain area will be cleared of mines to a certain depth. This risk appetite dovetails with the second leg of risk management in this context, the risk of the minefield after clearance. We shall return to this later.

When the required resources arrive, demining teams clear the mines according to rigidly defined standard operating procedures (SOPs – the IMAS referred to by Atkinson above). The procedures cover every aspect of mine clearance and every mine clearance technique, from rakes to rats (yes, really). For example, demining teams must mark minefields clearly and restrict access carefully; they must wear personal protective equipment correctly – 'If you leave your face mask up, you may as well not wear a helmet', says Atkinson – and it must be in good condition and appropriate to the expected mine types; deminers should work in mine clearance 'tracks' of standard width, take work breaks at standard intervals, drink water in standard quantities and so on.

Once the demining team has cleared a field, a different team samples the site to ensure that it is clear to the desired standard. The demining team documents the whole process and its results, and destroys the mines discovered. Finally, they must work with, inform and educate the local population. There are guidelines for all these processes too. The degree of standardization for demining recalls that for major incident management in earthquakes and the Standard Emergency Management System (SEMS – see chapter 9). In both cases risk is managed by training to and enforcing very rigorous standard operating procedures.

The extent to which deminers follow these procedures varies. In a 2005 report, GICHD noted that in its review of demining practices, 'no demining group was found to be in complete compliance with their own written SOPs'. This non-compliance may in part be the result of the progressive clearance of the most densely mined areas, leaving less dense, and hence less risky, fields to clear. Bjorsvik notes 'if you put people into areas where they find a mine every day, they pay attention. There are deminers out there who've been working for 10 years and have never found a mine. They get accustomed to the [lack of] risk.'

Cleared

Managing the risk to the local population after the aid activity is complete is in some respects harder than managing the risk to the aid workers, and involves some complex ethical judgements. For example as the densest minefields are cleared and attention turns to lower-risk areas, the environment starts to move from extreme to routine. In a routine environment, what is the appropriate level of residual risk? Traditionally, the view has been zero: every single ERW has to be dealt with.

Another view is that risks and costs should be balanced. Bjorsvik, on the leading edge of this discussion, explains:

Historically, we have been very conservative, risk averse. We cleared every piece of land. Now we want to release land much quicker than before. To us, the key question is 'What about the land you don't have to clear at all?' We want to move to a risk-based approach based on surveys rather than clearing every single piece of land.

Focusing his mind is NPA's current challenge in post-conflict south Sudan. 'The distances are huge: there are 11,000 kilometres of primary roads to clear, never mind the secondary ones. Even if we can't [clear and] open the roads, people will start using them anyway. It's an impossibly large task.' The task is magnified by the fact that 'the minefields were mostly laid by local military and paramilitary forces'. This means that '[the minefields] can be very low density', with a few mines scattered over a large area. The only way to deal with the situation is 'to accept some residual risk' and not attempt complete clearance for every kilometre of every road.

Bjorsvik feels that this risk-based approach is the right direction for humanitarian demining. For example:

> In 1994/95, a South African firm was contracted to clear mines in Mozambique. They cleared 2,500 kilometres of road and found 26 anti-tank mines. The Geneva Centre [GIHCD] did a rough estimate of the total number of mines found in all demining operations worldwide and divided by the total area cleared and found that 97 per cent of the land cleared had no mines. We spend too much time clearing clear ground.

Bjorsvik is promoting the use of risk-based surveying to drive risk-based clearance techniques. The higher the risk, the more detailed the survey, and vice versa. For example, his methodology would prescribe a full technical survey for strategic military 'hotspots' such as bridges and their immediate surroundings. If this survey finds the area to be high risk, clearance will be very thorough, consisting of 10 sweeps in an armoured vehicle (to detect anti-tank mines) with manual follow-up. In contrast, a stretch of road with no strategic value, no history of conflict, no remnants of war, and a clean bill of health from knowledgeable locals would not be surveyed or cleared at all. The final piece of the plan is to build a database to record the 'cumulative experience' of assessments, results and subsequent incidents to provide a fact base for policy going forward. This is a significant shift away from 'subjective risk management on site' – meaning that one individual takes the life and death decisions about who clears what and how they do it – which in any case is 'way too much responsibility for one person'.

The Achilles' heel in Bjorsvik's plan is liability. He worries about 'a bus load of American nurses that gets hit by a landmine', since 'we'd have a battalion of lawyers show up; we'd be sued all the way to the moon. There are no legal precedents in this area.' More generally, there is an ethical issue: should an aid agency expose local populations to a higher risk than would be acceptable to civilians from its home country? What if there are large potential rewards, such as permitting desperate recent returnees to plant their first crop? There are no good answers to these questions yet, nor a legal framework. As a result the application of such trade-offs may remain purely theoretical for some time, as the ethical, technical and liability issues are worked through. In the interim, 100 per cent clearance will remain the standard, and deminers will clear large areas that were already free of mines.

The key to *thinking* about risk in extreme aid environments is assessing the risk of deliberate harm to aid workers. This risk sets the boundary of aid organizations' risk tolerance. It follows from this risk that *planning* in these environments has two critical components: negotiating a non-intervention agreement with local armed parties, and setting up emergency evacuation plans in case they change their minds. If an aid agency cannot negotiate a non-intervention agreement, it should not start operations. These *thinking* and *planning* processes are similar to those used in terrorism and mountain risk management. The key risk management decision in all three cases is to assess incoming information on local conditions and act on it preventively if it looks bad, rather than waiting for the worst-case scenario to unfold.

Doing in this context means ensuring the physical health and safety of aid workers through a combination of secure facilities, security policies and readiness for evacuation. In demining operations, there are two additional aspects to *doing*. First is the rigorous application of standard operating procedures to the process of demining. Second is reaching a conclusion about how 'safe' a 'clear' area is, and communicating the residual risk effectively to the local population.

Continuously updating and communicating security assessments closes the loop between *doing* and *thinking*. Ensuring that there is a constant reference back to the original risk appetite should ensure that it does not get reset at escalating levels. 'Aid agencies hate to leave' says Owen. 'They have a hard time establishing their [risk] threshold. After four months in Malange I made it out for a break, then went back in. I wouldn't do that now.' The risk for aid workers is that of the unfortunate frog in a slowly heating pan of water – they don't feel the steady change in temperature and end up boiled. At the time of writing, war seems to be breaking out again in Sri Lanka. NPA is still active there, but is reconsidering its presence.

APPLICATIONS TO BUSINESS

Managing risk in an extreme aid environment has transferable lessons for business. There are certain transactions that businesses undertake only because they have some kind of guarantee to limit their potential losses. In most cases these are formal, legally binding guarantees stating that if a particular event occurs, the guarantor will step in and reimburse the business's losses. Insurance is exactly this sort of guarantee.

Sometimes these guarantees are less binding. For example, in certain markets it is fairly common to do a deal with one company on the basis of a 'soft' – that is, not legally binding – guarantee from a related company with which the bank has an extensive relationship. Another example would be to hedge a risky trading position with a second position whose price movements offset imperfectly those of the underlying position, and hence leave some residual risk.

Such partial, even implicit, protection can be valuable as long as the original relationships remain strong. There are two lessons from extreme aid. One is that if you ever feel that the relationship, personal or technical, has broken down, you should exit the deal or the position right now. For example, most investment managers' positions in the Russian oil and gas company Yukos relied on the assumption that the government would not investigate questionable business practices, such as tax evasion, committed under the previous regime. Without this implicit government support, Yukos was much less valuable. Exactly how much less valuable it was, the government demonstrated in 2005, as it drove Yukos into bankruptcy by suing for back taxes, then bought the productive assets in a rigged auction. Reliance on implicit government complicity remains part of most investment strategies in Russia. Such strategies remain vulnerable to similar events in the future.

The other lesson is that before you take on a position backed by an informal guarantee, you should make an evacuation plan. Before committing, figure out how you would get out of it if the guarantee disappeared. What would you do if the guarantor walked away from the deal? What would you do if the market regime changed and the hedge no longer offset your position? In particular, you should consider the scenario of 'evacuating to the airport as the rebels are coming into town'. The roads will be clogged: everyone else will be trying to do the same thing at the same time as you. In financial markets this is an aspect of the 'greater fool' theory: you think the asset is overpriced but you think you can unload it on a greater fool than yourself before its price falls. If you can't think of an escape route that doesn't depend on avoiding the traffic on the road to the airport – a greater fool – you probably shouldn't do the deal or take the position.

There is a more general application of these lessons. Once a deal is on the books, it becomes 'our deal' with a 'core relationship'. Behavioural economists call this the 'endowment effect', meaning that you apply a different set of criteria to something after you own it than you did before you bought it. Think about all the random objects cluttering your storage spaces at home. Their very location makes it apparent you don't need them, but you can't bring yourself to part with them. The upshot is that risk managers often hear the argument that even though a deal has deteriorated and wouldn't be accepted as it now stands, the organization has it and should live with it; it probably can't get worse, can't it? In recent years these discussions have centred on US car companies and airlines; one imagines that there must have been plenty of such discussions in Japanese banks during the 1990s. This too is a form of risk appetite resetting. Risk managers must always keep the overall risk appetite in sight, and apply it consistently through time and space.

Another cross-over is from demining specifically. Demining is risky, but if it is performed professionally the risk can be managed down to acceptable levels. This means sticking rigidly to the procedures. Businesses such as leveraged finance or sub-prime consumer lending are intrinsically high risk. The risk can be managed down through the rigid application of credit and operational standards. Risk managers in these businesses apply strict standards – limits on debt levels relative to equity, interest payments relative to cash flow, 'material adverse change' clauses in contracts that enforce repayment of debt if there is a takeover for example, credit quality acceptance thresholds, and so on – for this reason. The rules are there for a purpose: to protect the institution. Bending them will lead to the institution ending up in the financial services equivalent of a minefield without a map. However attractive it looks to relax the rules, you stray from them at your peril.

The current debate around managing the residual risk to local populations from 'cleared' minefields is an excellent case study in thinking through the implications of adopting a risk appetite and implementing it operationally. If the expected gain from incremental mine clearance is very small and the cost is very large, under certain circumstances it may not be worth it. Equally, small expected gains from incremental risk analysis may not be worth if they come at high cost. Most financial institutions spend a lot of time and money analysing low-risk deals for low-risk customers. It is not clear that this expense is worthwhile, since the loss avoided is often less than the cost of analysis.

There is also a direct application in country risk. Businesses may want to pitch for business in high-risk countries. As a first step, it would make sense to consider who, if anyone, could provide credible and sustained protection to employees in-country, and how they could be persuaded to do so.

Arguably the regular violent kidnaps of oil workers in the Niger Delta at the time of writing are an illustration of the breakdown of historic security guarantees provided to oil companies there. The national government can no longer guarantee security. There is no replacement power to negotiate with, as local communities are fragmenting as interest groups proliferate to claim a share in the extortion revenue.

Oil companies, unlike aid agencies, cannot simply withdraw since they have billions of dollars of investment at stake. At present they are suspending production ('shutting in' the oil) from certain wells as a temporary measure. As a result, they look likely to retreat behind ever more restrictive rules for employees, coupled with protection payments to an increasing number of hostile local actors. It's not clear how this will play out in the long term, but the prognosis isn't good.

In the next chapter we analyse risk management in another environment where those at risk are voluntarily exposed, the mountains.

5

Mountain

Interviewees

Stéphane Bozon	Captain, Péloton de la Gendarmerie d'Haute Montagne (PGHM, the mountain rescue service), Chamonix-Mont Blanc, France
Nick Banks	Owner, Mountain Tracks Guiding, Chamonix, France
Davy Gunn	Team leader, Glencoe Mountain Rescue, Scotland
Mike Grocott	Consultant physician at the Whittington Hospital in London, UK

Captain Stéphane Bozon of the Péloton de la Gendarmerie d'Haute Montagne (PGHM, the mountain rescue service) of Chamonix-Mont Blanc in France has lost a number of friends over the years. Recently, he lost one more:

> My friend was rescuing a couple of climbers, a man and a woman, one of whom was injured, from the top of a high pillar. The weather was OK. My friend went up with the helicopter to get them. He was winched down from the helicopter to the top of the pillar. As [the top of the pillar] was quite flat and wide, he didn't tie on [to the pillar]. He hooked up the first climber, and she was winched up to the helicopter safely, no problem. The [winch] hook came back down and my friend hooked the second climber on. As the cable took the load and went taut, the climber span round suddenly. On the back of his pack [the climber] had an ice pick. The pick caught my friend here [Bozon grabs the lower hem of his fleece] and he was lifted up too. Unfortunately it didn't hold, and the next instant he fell.

Looking like he's been punched in the stomach, Bozon continued 'He should have tied on, and he should have checked the climber's backpack. We've now made these checks mandatory.'

Not only rescuers die in the mountains. According to Bozon, 70 people were killed in the mountains of Haute-Savoie, the province where Chamonix-Mont Blanc is located, in 2004 – more than on the roads. This environment is unusual among extreme environments in that it is not hierarchical: there is no central power that can prevent determined climbers from climbing or skiers from skiing. Indeed, for them, danger is part of the attraction. Joe Simpson, experienced climber and author of the celebrated novel *Touching the Void* (1998), articulates this as 'The defining thing about climbing is that it kills you.' Consequently, the role of the 'authorities', in this case the PGHM, is to supply the best possible information about hazards and to make a good-faith, last-resort search and rescue effort. The rest of risk management in this environment is up to the individual climber, skier or expedition.

AVALANCHE

Nick Banks, a 30-something mountain guide bleached and crisped by weeks on the glaciers, has worked in Chamonix for two decades. Since his life will be one of those at risk if an accident occurs, he takes the daily guidance from the PGHM very seriously. He incorporates the information into his route planning, as, unlike Bozon, he has some control over his location and the timing of events. From his point of view, the single most important part of his risk management process is knowing when to say 'no'.

He speaks from experience:

Seven or eight years ago I was guiding a group of seven very skilled clients. We'd had poor snow all week, so on the last day we headed to Sainte Foy, a small resort with a big north-facing bowl that I thought might have some untracked snow. I checked with the ski patrol when I got there. They said the snow wasn't great, that there had been high winds, and that the [slopes with] north-east aspects were dodgy. I figured that it should be possible to get some good skiing without having to use north-east-facing slopes, so we skinned up [fixed a climbing 'skin' to the bottom of the ski to make it possible to 'walk' uphill] and started climbing.

We got to the bowl after about two hours skinning, but there were already some other skiers there. I really wanted to give the clients some fresh tracks, so we skinned on for another 15 minutes. It was a bit more north-east-facing, but not too much.

> The entrance to the bowl at this point was very steep. I went down on a rope and tested the snow pack.

He did this by cutting through several layers of snow to see how they were holding together. Layers of snow that are not firmly stuck together are likely to slide apart and cause an avalanche. Banks concluded that:

> It seemed OK. The visibility was good. I looked down the slope and thought, if there was an avalanche, what would happen? It was a long, wide slope, quite even, no rocks, hollows or cliffs, so it looked to me like an avalanche would move slowly and probably peter out before it got too far. For sure there should be time to get out of the way.
>
> I gave the signal, and the others roped down to where I was. I explained that there was a moderate avalanche risk, and that they should stay within [the span of] my tracks. I led with big swing turns across the slope to cut the snow [to break the crust and release any latent avalanches]. When I got to the bottom of the first pitch everything seemed fine, so I signalled to the rest of the party to go ahead, two at a time. Then I skied on.

At this point, Banks takes a breath and sips his water.

> The fifth man down went slightly outside my tracks and into a gully that was invisible from the top of the slope – and full of windblown snow. His movement caused a slab [of snow] to break off and slide down the gully, taking the whole slope with it. [The avalanche] was 50 metres wide when it hit me. I was taken completely unawares: it was all powder snow, completely silent; I didn't hear a thing.
>
> Four of us were buried in the avalanche. Luckily nobody was badly hurt, but it really shook me up. I would probably do the same again, but I pushed it right up to the limit. It could have been the end of me.

This is a surprising conclusion perhaps, but Banks went through all the appropriate checks at all the appropriate points, and he feels that this saved his life and those of his clients.

Davy Gunn, team leader at Glencoe Mountain Rescue in Scotland, had the opposite experience: in position immediately above a gully where an avalanche had trapped three climbers, Gunn wanted to proceed but his colleagues held him back. A couple of seconds later, even as Gunn continued to argue, a second avalanche swept past them down the gully. The delay probably saved all their lives.

The broader point is that risk management is just that: management. You can manage risk, but not eliminate it. With good risk management you improve your odds of survival, but in extreme environments there are no guarantees.

FREEDOM TO DIE

Climbers and skiers are their own primary risk managers. *Thinking* about risk in the mountains means setting a risk appetite in terms of the difficulty of the objectives. Implicitly this degree of difficulty relates the frequency and severity of accidents. Different climbs are helpfully graded from easy to extreme by various national and regional climbing organizations. In addition to this formal assessment, it is imperative to get an up-to-date risk assessment of any given objective from local mountain guides or the PGHM. Of particular importance is an update on avalanche risk, since this varies locally as a result of the exact sequence of weather conditions – amount and type of snow, speed and direction of wind, sunshine and temperature – in each location.

Mike Grocott, a consultant physician at the Whittington Hospital in London, a specialist in extreme medicine and the lead researcher on a 2006 Everest expedition, notes that the overall risk of mountaineering has diminished because of better equipment – everything from Gore-tex to satellite phones – and more professional planning. 'It's not the Duke of so-and-so any more', he quips. Despite this, fatality rates have stayed more or less constant in the range of 1 to 3%. It appears that mountaineers may simply take more risk to compensate for the risk mitigation.

Planning then means matching the experience, skill and fitness of the mountaineers to the difficulty of their objectives under the expected conditions. An honest assessment is critical, otherwise mountaineers may simply fall off the mountain.

Assuming that the party's ability matches the difficulty of the object-ive, they can then *plan* the logistics. The trade-off between speed, load and technique is central. For example, Grocott notes that the primary style of mountaineering has changed fundamentally, from 'Himalayan-style' expeditions with numerous porters and voluminous equipment, to 'Alpine style', where individuals or small groups climb and descend quickly, carrying 'tiny loads' of the bare minimum of supplies. The quickest solution is to go without ropes at all, and paradoxically there is a risk management aspect to this as 'the quicker you climb the shorter your exposure'. Conversely, minimizing equipment means that there is no safety margin, and if a problem occurs, the climbers are more vulnerable.

In addition, aggressive climbing means fewer, faster safety checks and procedures, so all other things being equal, there is a higher probability of an accident. Most extreme mountaineers opt for speed, carrying a minimal load in order to minimize the time during which they are at highest risk. For extraordinarily fit and capable people, this is probably appropriate; for everyone else it's extraordinarily risky.

The other requirements before setting out are training, reconnaissance and acclimatization. The party should spend time getting used to the altitude, familiarizing themselves with their route, local landmarks and weather patterns, and practising relevant techniques.

In doing so, the most important decision is whether or not to go out. This is especially true if the conditions are bad, as most ascents and descents are orders of magnitude easier in good weather. If the weather is too bad, the expedition should not set out. What might be a simple climb in good weather can be transformed by wind, cold, rain and darkness.

Once a group is under way, the group must revisit this decision periodically. The key is to be honest about how changes in the conditions and health may make an objective unattainable, thereby recognizing the increase in risk relative to the original risk appetite.

One mechanism for enforcing this recognition is to commit to the conditions under which a group will change route or turn back, and decide if they do so, how they will do it. At its simplest, this means 'If we haven't got to the summit by 2 pm, we turn back [and retrace our steps].' This also sounds easy, but in practice it's hard to say no when the summit is close by. John Krakauer's Book *Into Thin Air* (1998) gives a harrowing account of 11 deaths that occurred on Everest on a single day in 1996, because several groups stayed on the mountain past their turning-back time and a bad storm blew in. There is always a temptation to view changes incrementally – just a little bit colder, wetter or more tired – and therefore as being manageable. 'It's important not to be the frog in the saucepan and slowly boil to death', says Banks.

The other major risk on the mountain is injury or ill-health. If the issue arises before departure, the party should consider not setting out. If it happens en route, the party should activate their contingency plan, typically to call for a helicopter and evacuate. Again, the more extreme the conditions and the farther from civilization, the harder this is and the more useful a tactical reserve of food and equipment might be.

NO HOLIDAY ALLOWANCE

Rescuers *think* about risk in a fundamentally different way from most of those they rescue. Rescuers live in the mountains. They have no holiday allowance to use up, can ski or climb all through the season, and hence have no reason to take extraordinary risks on any given day. They also know that they are at the sharp end every day. If they don't manage their risk, they will surely suffer. Recreational climbers and skiers usually have only a limited amount of time available. As a result, there is always the temptation to proceed with an expedition, even if the conditions look bad. They may implicitly accept a higher risk appetite.

Free of the time constraints faced by most climbers and skiers, and regularly exposed to injuries and deaths, Bozon believes that his team have strong motivation to manage their risks themselves. Once the team is convinced that the mission is feasible, a carefully planned rescue by a team with the right skills and equipment should not result in casualties. His particular concern is to make sure that events do not compound: that is, build up one on top of another. Chains of events – a climber gets hurt, the wind strengthens, the winch stops working, a rescuer gets hit by lightning and so on – cause the 'multiplication' of risk and are at the centre of most of the worst accidents.

Grocott takes the same view of risk multiplication but from a medical point of view:

> After rock and ice falls and avalanches, the next greatest danger on an Everest ascent is the final ridge. Climbers are extremely vulnerable due to a combination of oxygen deprivation, exhaustion and exposure. Since at altitude everyone is more disposed to infection, and any acute infection – such as diarrhoea – increases the chances of altitude sickness and exhaustion, we follow obsessively a personal hygiene protocol, including handwashing with permanganate.

Bozon ensures that his teams plan missions carefully before they set out, combining the right number of rescuers with the right mix equipment for the number of people to be rescued, their medical condition, the location and the weather conditions. The plan is revised when the team can see the accident. The final authority to proceed with the rescue rests with the team on site: if not all team members are convinced that the rescue can be conducted at acceptable risk, the mission is called off. Gunn concurs: 'You have to put together a plan before you set out, but often the early information is all wrong. You have to be dynamic.'

When it comes to *doing*, Bozon, a dark, wiry man in his early 40s, chooses only very skilled, experienced individuals who have experienced extreme conditions. All his gendarmes are qualified as both mountain infantry and mountain guides. Maintaining these qualifications imposes a heavy training burden. Beyond these requirements, Bozon adds training exercises. His aim is to 'make the stress of a rescue an everyday experience'. Training exercises take place once a month during the off season in the most challenging and dangerous terrain in the valley, albeit typically in 'decent' weather. Combined with the experience accumulated through numerous actual rescues, the PGHM provides an intense environment for individual and group development. The gendarmes are accustomed to operating in extreme circumstances, and as a result they are able to manage the risks involved in high mountain rescues effectively.

This approach is shared by other mountain rescue teams. Gunn looks for strong climbing skills. 'Rescues are technical, so we need technical climbers,' he says. He also drives his team members to improve. In his view 'knowledge is power – if we practise what we have to do, where we have to do it, then we should stay in control'. Since they have no helicopters, they have 'no excuses' and operate in all weather conditions. 'We climb steep mountains in bad weather, because that's what we do [when we're called out]. Rescue is dangerous', he says. Glencoe's training programme covers not only climbing technique and equipment use but also endurance: one requirement is to spend 24 hours above 12,500 feet once a year.

Bozon also closes the loop between *doing* and *thinking* by driving a continuous improvement programme based on a detailed review of each mission. Every aspect, good and bad, of a mission is evaluated, and potential improvements to training or equipment are identified. Near misses, where an accident did not happen but might have, receive an especially close look. Bozon cites the development of special procedures to manage the critical moment when the rescuer is attached simultaneously to both the ground and the helicopter, and the steady improvement in the strength-to-weight ratio of their helicopter winching equipment as a result of suggestions made through this process. (Standard policy is for rescuers to tie themselves onto the rock face while they are still attached to the winch. This reduces the risk of falling as they are always attached to something. It also means that for a short period the helicopter is tethered to the rock face too.) Recommendations from Bozon's group also make their way into the French mountain rescue standard procedures and training through the Centre Nationale d'Instruction de Ski et Alpinisme de la Gendarmerie (CNISAG, pronounced 'sneezag'), located down the street in Chamonix.

The gendarmes also try to manage their risks by influencing the *thinking* and *planning*, and hence the behaviour, of participants. Every day they publish guidance for guides and mountaineers, outlining the major risks in the Chamonix area (rock falls, snow falls, avalanches, snow and ice accumulations, flash flood warnings, storm warnings, etc). In 2003 they went further. Since a massive heat wave had resulted in more or less continuous rock and ice falls on a section of the route up Mont Blanc, they stationed a gendarme at the entry point to the traverse to 'ensure that climbers were fully informed of the risks'. Most turned back.

The mountain environment is unique among the extreme environments in this book in that mountaineering is a leisure activity. Like humanitarian aid it is pursued by independent actors with predominantly non-economic motives. Participation is entirely voluntary, and the majority of participants are fully aware of the risks they take – indeed the risks themselves are part of the attraction. It is also unique in that the 'authorities' cannot in general restrict access to the mountains.

Consequently, unlike a location prone to natural disasters, there is no social contract between state and citizen that offers succour in return for compliance. Instead, there is a local bargain whereby local search and rescue teams provide as good a service as the local community can afford. Mountaineers cannot rely on being rescued in the same way or to the same extent as citizens in an earthquake zone or workers down a mine. Paradoxically – at least from a rational risk management point of view – this possibility of not being rescued makes an ascent more appealing to hard-core mountaineers.

Both rescuers and participants agree, then, on the keys to managing risk in the mountains. First is *thinking* clearly so that you can say 'no' when things change and the risks move beyond your risk appetite. If you plan an expedition that is within your capabilities in good weather but bad weather descends, don't start out. If the weather worsens en route, or the temperature rises suddenly, increasing avalanche risk materially, turn back. Equally, if you plan an expedition that needs five healthy people and two get sick, wait for them to get better. Don't go out with three fit people, or perhaps worse, with three fit and two sick people. It is always tempting to proceed, especially if you are pursuing a 'trophy' objective such as a first ascent, and even more so if you have a limited period of time to do so. However, knowing when to say 'no' can mean the difference between life and death.

Second, avoid compound events by anticipating the various events that might happen and *planning* around them. Compound events are the generators of worst-case scenarios. Each individual event is itself not fatal, but the collective effect can be catastrophic. Risk managers need to deconstruct the sources of risk and plan for each one, so that the group can cope with individual component failures before they have a chance to compound. For example, the group might decide to carry two copies of mission-critical equipment, to take four days' fuel even if they only expect to be out for two days, or to take a party of six people even if they only really need five. In addition, groups require adherence to rigid checking procedures prior to starting out, similar to those used routinely by pilots prior to take-off. Very high risk undertakings tend to rely on procedures rather than equipment, since reducing weight carried increases endurance and flexibility.

Third, train to match your skills and physical condition to the task you want to achieve. Train to the level of the challenges you expect to encounter. Do not attempt Everest if you can't manage Ben Nevis.

Fourth, keep your head if the worst happens: 'Don't make yourself a casualty.' You might be rescued, but since the rescue team are only human and helicopters can't fly in very bad weather, you shouldn't count on it.

APPLICATION TO BUSINESS

The principles of risk management in the mountains are transferable to business settings. For example, as noted in Chapter 3, sometimes investment banks will postpone the flotation of a client company on a stock exchange because of market turbulence. Harsher conditions have increased the risk of the flotation beyond their risk appetite. Postponement is embarrassing, but better than taking a big loss. This is directly analogous to bad weather delaying a mountaineering expedition: postponement is frustrating, but it beats dying.

Many mountaineers do not feel they have the option to postpone, however. They only spend part of their time in the mountains. When faced with hazardous conditions, they think about the money they have spent in getting to the mountains and, given their limited vacation time, how long it might be before they come back, and they say to themselves, 'What they heck, let's do it.' They go off up into the mountains into conditions that are over their risk appetite, and most of the time they get away with it, but one day they never come back.

This is analogous to the 'sunk cost fallacy' in investment decisions. Sunk cost is the amount of money you have already spent on a project. If something unexpected happens well into a project, there's a temptation to continue regardless rather than 'waste' all the money already spent. After all, it might turn out all right.

The launch of the space shuttle *Challenger* in 1986 is a good example of this phenomenon. The temperature on the launch site was far below any previous launch. Engineers raised concerns about safety. NASA decided to go ahead. The programme had coped with plenty of unknowns over the years, and the agency had too much at stake to cancel the whole programme. In retrospect, their stated risk appetite was far below the risks they were routinely running with the shuttle launches. The physicist Richard Feynman noted that:

It appears that there are enormous differences of opinion as to the probability of a failure with loss of vehicle and of human life. The estimates range from roughly 1 in 100 to 1 in 100,000. The higher figures come from the working engineers, and the very low figures from management.

Since rare events are rare, the agency got away with having a higher risk appetite than it had stated publicly for a long time. On this occasion its luck ran out.

If conditions have changed so much that a project is no longer worthwhile looking forward, you should terminate the project now, irrespective of how much money's already been sunk into it. You will never be able to get the money already spent back, so it shouldn't have any bearing on your decisions going forward. If conditions have worsened so much that you can't realistically attain your objective, don't think about the money already spent to get you there, because it can't change the weather for you right now.

Most examples in business are not as dramatic as the *Challenger* disaster. Rather they are drawn-out sagas of overruns and serial restructurings like the Channel Tunnel, which spent 19 years sliding into bankruptcy; or the London Stock Exchange's Taurus electronic trading platform, which was eventually abandoned in 1993 after seven years in development and $100 million in direct costs.

Another lesson for business it that you shouldn't undertake risky activities without the necessary expertise. Risky activities by their nature offer high profits in good years: high rewards stem from high risks. Many organizations are tempted during these good years to enter risky businesses. However, these businesses require specialized skills. In financial markets, those who lack these skills tend to end up on the wrong end of a process called adverse selection. Adverse selection is when a firm ends up with a systematically riskier portfolio than it expected. It happens like this. The new entrant arrives in the market and pitches for business. It wins business by either offering lower prices or banking new clients. Unfortunately, the business it wins is usually the business that the established, better informed firms don't want because it's very risky, so the new entrants end up with a portfolio of underpriced risks. In North America, established firms call such a new entrants 'stuffees': that is, the party that gets 'stuffed', ripped off, on a deal.

When the good years end, such portfolios are hit hard. Leveraged lending in the United States is a risky business. A number of foreign banks active in this market in the United States in the late 1990s, including the Industrial Bank of Japan (now part of Mizuho) and Dresdner (now part of Allianz), experienced exactly this dynamic and lost large amounts of money as the risk in their portfolio crystallized during the 2000–01 slowdown. Other banks expanded in Latin America in the early 1990s only to withdraw by the early 2000s. The lesson here is to train to the level of your ambition. Risky ventures are not easy. Enter high-risk markets cautiously, with realistic growth targets, and ideally a partner who knows the market well as well.

In the next chapter we shall discuss risk management in nuclear power, focusing on the largest nuclear power accident in history, Chernobyl.

6

Meltdown

Interviewees

Andrey Zinienko	Formerly chief electrical engineer, Chernobyl nuclear plant, Ukraine; now consultant to Shelter Project
Alexander Knyshevich	Formerly deputy head of the reactor operations, reactors 5 and 6, Chernobyl nuclear plant, Ukraine; now consultant to Shelter Project
Jeremy Western	Director of environment and liabilities, British Energy, UK
Georgi Reihktmann	Formerly engineer shift head on the reactors 3 and 4, Chernobyl nuclear plant, Ukraine; now consultant to Shelter Project
Nikolai Steinberg	Formerly deputy chief engineer, Chernobyl nuclear plant, Ukraine (after the accident); now Deputy Minister for Power and Fuel, Ukraine
Nigel Holloway	UK Atomic Energy Authority

At 1.23 am on 26 April 1986, one of the four operational nuclear reactors at the Chernobyl plant in Ukraine exploded during a safety test. The explosion caused the largest release of radioactive materials in civilian history and killed thousands.[1]

---

[1] Thirty-one deaths resulted directly from the explosion and its immediate aftermath. On this there is agreement. Beyond this, estimates vary from a few dozen to half a million. In 2005 the United Nations and International Atomic Energy Authority (IAEA) revised down their estimate to 4,000 incremental deaths from cancer. This is 3 to 4% of total expected cancer deaths.

'I had fallen asleep reading a book when I got a call. From the ring tone I knew it was the plant,' said Andrey Zinienko, the chief electrical engineer of the Chernobyl nuclear power plant at the time of the accident:

> It was my deputy. It was a couple of minutes after the accident. He said 'You need to come here at once, we have a radiation emission.' He said he already had breathing apparatus on and was taking tablets. I told my family that there had been a serious accident. My wife asked me when I would be back. I thought it was a local problem, confined to the plant, and did not think it would take long to resolve. I didn't tell her to stay indoors or pack, anything like that.
>
> A car came to pick me up at 2 am. As we drove over the railway bridge, I saw that the night sky above the plant was red. I knew then it was serious, so when I arrived I called my wife and told her to close the windows.

Alexander Knyshevich was the deputy head of the reactor operations 'shop' for the unfinished reactors 5 and 6. His first reaction when he heard about the accident was to drive in with his son to see what was going on. 'As I went over the railway bridge I saw that something was wrong with the fourth [reactor], so I turned round and took my son home.'

Zinienko continues:

> Reactors 1, 2 and 3 were in normal operation. However there was no power at all in the control room for number 4. This meant that the power facilities were damaged, the reserve power also. I went outside to have a look, and there was a heavy smell of ozone, graphite everywhere. I could tell that the damage was serious. After 15 minutes outside I felt sick, and I thought I might faint, so I went to the underground shelter. As the sun rose, I went back outside to find out why there was no reserve power. I found a cable on top of the transformer, so I arranged for its repair. The repair team got a big dose of radiation, as they were right in front of the damaged reactor.
>
> On 27 April, the second day, the evacuation was announced. My family was sent away... we all realized the full extent of the accident.

Very few others did. The Soviet government did not release any information to the public for several days, perhaps not wanting to spoil the parades due for 1 May. 'It was the sort of regime where the life of one person was worth less than an idea', says one survivor. Rumours abounded of the elite sending their families away. 'There was a kind of panic. Every train [from nearby Kiev] to every destination was sold out.'

Jeremy Western, director of environment and liabilities at nuclear firm British Energy, noted this lack of openness on his visit to Chernobyl in 1988:

The regime was completely incomprehensible. There was no safety culture at all. For example, there was only one copy of the emergency plan on the station, since photocopiers could be used for political purposes and weren't allowed. The local doctor wasn't trained to recognize that vomiting was a sign of radiation sickness... there was such compartmentalization of information. This was very dangerous technology made very vulnerable, since barriers were erected that prevented the spread of the knowledge necessary to develop a safety culture.

LIQUIDATION

The Soviet authorities set up a State Commission to take control of the 'liquidation' of the accident. Likely drawing on plans for civil defence in case of a nuclear missile attack, they evacuated every resident within 30 kilometres, extinguished the fire, sealed the damaged reactor inside the 'object shelter', a concrete and steel sarcophagus, and finally decontaminated the site. Approximately 600,000 people were involved, among them Zinienko, Knyshevich, Reihktmann and Steinberg (see below).

Outlining his role in the liquidation, Knyshevich continues:

There was a technical survey of reactor 4, and we realized the scale of the accident and of what needed to be done. The most important issue was the evacuation of the population from Pripyat [the company town where all the staff lived]. They took less than 24 hours to make a decision. Hundreds of buses arrived in Pripyat on the 27th, and by 2 pm there was nobody left.

We fought the fire with water, then nitrogen gas to choke it and stop the graphite burning. We were fully suited up: breathing apparatus, radiation detectors, the lot. For four days helicopters dropped lead and sand onto the damaged reactor through the [hole in the] roof. The State Committee thought there was a possibility of the reactor burning through the base of the reactor compartment, and of radioactive substances getting into the groundwater. We built an underground tunnel from reactor number 3 under the fourth reactor to carry cooling water, and heat protection was constructed using the graphite tiles. Once the situation was stabilized at the fourth unit, we went through the process of separating [reactors] 3 and 4 – water, ventilation and so on.

The situation was under control in the first 24 hours. It was an accident but nothing extraordinary.

This is a surprising turn of phrase in the circumstances. The meltdown of the reactor core and the leakage of radiation continued for several more days. The evacuation caused massive disruption. There were 115,000 people displaced from the 30 km exclusion zone around the plant. There used to be 47,000 people living in Pripyat, the company town. Today nobody does; it is empty, silent. At the plant itself, radioactivity inside the sarcophagus – a death mask, really – is still sufficient to kill someone in less than 10 minutes. It will remain at unsafe levels for thousands of years. Immediately outside, workers creating a new sarcophagus (an object shelter for the object shelter, as it were) can work for only 20 minutes a day. Even at a safe distance of 200 metres, Geiger counters chirp continuously.

AN IMPOSSIBILITY

Many of the causes of the accident at Chernobyl stemmed from the way that people at all levels thought about the risk in the system. To them, an event like this was simply impossible.

Georgi Reihktmann is a physicist and former nuclear submarine officer. At the time of the accident he was engineer shift head on the nuclear 'shop'. Like the other interviewees:

> On the day of the accident I had a day off in Pripyat. We hadn't heard anything [about the accident]. My brother was in town and he said 'You must be very rich here, if you wash the streets with washing powder.' Rationally, I knew that this was decontamination, and that something bad must have happened, but I did nothing about it. I should have gone home and closed the windows and so on, but it just didn't register. Later the same day I was at the garage and someone said that something bad had happened. We discussed it, but no one thought that the reactor might have blown. My son played football all day within sight of the burning reactor.
>
> At university we were told that a reactor couldn't be damaged. Everyone was sure that this couldn't happen. I guess you shouldn't always believe what you're taught.

Nikolai Steinberg, who became the deputy chief engineer of the plant after the accident and is now Ukraine's deputy minister for power and fuel, says flatly: 'People implemented technology they couldn't control.' He looks down at his fingertips for a moment, then looks back up and continues, his eyes flashing: 'Never again.'

Things have changed, he says. Going forward:

Our aim is to make nuclear power safe for the mass market – so safe that a nuclear power plant could be located anywhere, without restriction. In fact we have already achieved the level of safety required for this but we have to demonstrate it to the public. What was too expensive or impossible 10 years ago is now common practice… nuclear reactors get safer over time.

For example, he says, 'Sizewell B is not the same as Windscale', referring to the youngest and oldest nuclear reactors in the United Kingdom, started up in 1994 and 1950 respectively. (The name of Windscale was subsequently changed to Sellafield.)

The perception of risk is as critical as the reality. 'Ukrainians get twice as much aggregate radiation from [fossil fuel] power plants as from nuclear plants,' says Steinberg:

[However] people assume nuclear power is unsafe – perhaps because the first implementation of nuclear power was for the bombs at Hiroshima and Nagasaki. It may be that it is tainted forever. Moreover, everyone understands burning coal to create energy, whereas people think that nuclear power is basically magic.

Western agrees. 'Nuclear power stations are portrayed as mysterious – you only ever see them on TV, with scary music.' People know that flying is dangerous but since most people have flown or know someone who has, it is familiar. 'This [familiarity] creates a feeling that they can make a judgement on their safety. We would like to provide opportunities to gain the same familiarity with nuclear plants, but given the security situation it's hard.'

AS LOW AS REASONABLY PRACTICABLE

Today nuclear operators are very explicit in the way they think about risk. Western continues:

We developed the 'tolerability of risk' framework [in the United Kingdom] for the Sizewell B enquiry. Basically the enquiry asked 'How do you decide whether something is safe enough?' [The outcome was that] if you could show that the probability of death of a member of the public from a particular cause exceeds 1 in 10,000 per year, that's an intolerable level of risk whatever the benefits you provide. At less than 1 in 1 million, it's acceptable and you won't be pushed by regulators to reduce it further, unless to do so is easy. In practice this means that if the risk to the public from your enterprise is above 1 in 10,000 years, the regulators will insist you reduce it – there is no way you'll receive a permit. For the range in between this and 1 in 1 million we apply the principle of ALARP – as low as reasonably practicable.

In this ALARP range cost–benefit analysis is applied so that any measure where the cost of reducing risk further is not 'grossly disproportionate' to the improvement in safety has to be implemented. The risk assessment must also allow for 'common mode failures', where more than one safety system fails at the same time. To be conservative, Western says, 'We don't allow claims of reliability for any system above 1 in 10,000.'

Steinberg emphasizes the commonality in approach, without committing to a specific risk appetite:

> Risk management here [in the Ukraine] is like risk management elsewhere, there is no difference. We use the same 'risk equals probability times consequences' concept. When you apply this in the nuclear industry, it is clear that the primary risks are to health and the environment. Your analysis of these risks determines whether you build or not. If you think they are manageable, you look at the expense.

Moving on to planning, Western continues:

> For a big project, we identify all the events that could initiate an accident, and then all the subsequent individual fault sequences that could lead to a loss of radiation to the atmosphere. For example, the loss of offsite power. We then group these 'release events' into buckets by the size of the release, and [for each bucket] convert this to an overall loss number covering deaths, cancer, evacuation and abandonment.

This loss number feeds into the risk tolerability calculations. At Chernobyl, a release was officially impossible, so these calculations were not performed.

Nigel Holloway of the UK Atomic Energy Authority (UKAEA) points at a foot-high stack of documents in the corner of his office, and says:

> See that? Those 10,000 pages cover only the risks of a reactor in the shutdown state. The documents that cover the risks of an operational reactor are much longer.
>
> The [risk management] process identifies and measures every risk [event] in every reactor state using fault trees, then assigns probabilities

---

A fault tree is a recursive tree diagram tracing all the possible causes of a fault, and the causes of the causes, the causes of the causes of the causes, and so on.

and consequences to each one. For example, we might look at the risk [to operators] from handling plutonium by breaking it down into: the probability of getting cut; the likely size of the wound; the dose [of radiation]; the absorption coefficient into the blood stream; and the probability of dying from the dose. Sometimes you have all this data, sometimes you estimate. We try to control each risk up to the point where it is acceptable. This is usually interpreted as an expected probability of death of 10 to the minus six [1 in 1 million]. Ten to the minus four [1 in 10,000] would be regarded as intolerable.

'Reactors are designed to resist disasters', he goes on. However, there are certain events, such as a direct hit by a large civil airliner or military jet at full speed, that 'might not breach the reactor containment but would destroy everything else', including the cooling system:

> [For a PWR] we'd have a couple of hours to respond before the fuel melted and radioactivity escaped. We've estimated the likelihood of this at 10 to the minus seven to 10 to the minus eight [1 in 10 million to 1 in 100 million].

Thinking and *planning* are closely linked. A nuclear reactor is not natural. The probabilities and consequences of events in a nuclear reactor are driven by design and procedural choices, intentional and unintentional. Unintentional design choices typically emerge from unexpected combinations of intentional choices. A particularly important intentional design choice is that all currently operating nuclear power reactors are designed so that as the power output goes up, the rate of nuclear fission in the core goes down. This is called negative reactivity feedback. The reactor at Chernobyl did not have this feature. Without it, fission can increase with increased power, and an uncontrolled chain reaction can occur. In a pressurised water reactor (PWR), negative reactivity feedback comes from the use of water as a moderator (see box).

More generally, designers try to engineer safety into the system. One example of engineering safety is the use of electromagnetism to hold control rods in position. These are rods of neutron-absorbing material that can be raised from or lowered into the reactor to control the rate of neutron flow and hence the rate of the nuclear reaction. If electrical power is cut, the magnets will fail and the control rods will fall into the reactor under gravity. Designers also use redundancy to provide higher levels of safety. Redundancy means multiple copies of the same component, so that if the primary fails, the secondary copy can function in its place. Most reactor designs, for example, include multiple copies of critical components such as pumps.

Western notes that 'neither Three Mile Island nor Chernobyl were designed using this approach. [These days] you design out the reactivity problems.' With some understatement, he continues, 'The rest is the safety culture.' Together these kinds of features make reactors that are 'in some ways simple, in some ways complex. It is easy to shut one down, harder to keep it critical.'

Positive feedback in PWRs

Nuclear power is driven by atomic fission – splitting atoms. This occurs when atoms of a particular type of uranium (U-235) are hit by neutrons and break up. Each break-up releases energy, in the form of heat and gamma rays (a type of radiation), and more neutrons. For the chain reaction to continue, the released neutrons must hit other U-235 atoms. In general the neutrons released are moving too fast to be readily absorbed by other atoms. Moderators are substances that slow down the neutrons enough so that they are absorbed and fission can continue. In PWRs, the moderator is water. At Chernobyl it was graphite, hence Zinienko's comment about the 'graphite everywhere' after the explosion. Graphite moderates (that is, slows) neutrons more than water.

The interaction between water volume and density at high temperatures and pressures means that if the reactivity of the core goes up, its temperature goes up. If the core temperature goes up, the temperature of the water in the cooling system goes up. If the temperature of the water goes up, so does its volume. As the volume of water goes up its density goes down, and as its density goes down, the water slows fewer neutrons. Faster-moving neutrons are less likely to be absorbed by uranium atoms, and so the reactivity of the core goes down. Using water as both coolant and moderator is an example of trying to design in 'inherent safety'. If the water leaks, the chain reaction will slow down even as the coolant disappears. This still leaves the problem of residual decay heat – a nuclear reactor cannot be completely switched off – but shutting down the reactor gives more time to respond.

The control rods at Chernobyl offer a good illustration of an unintentional design choice. The tips of the control rods were graphite. The next metre was hollow and filled with water. The rest of the rods were boron carbide, a substance that absorbs neutrons and hence slows nuclear reactions. The operators had fully withdrawn the rods to maintain power output for the safety test. When reactivity spiked, the operators reinserted the rods to try to shut down the reactor. However, in that critical first moment of re-entry, water in the reactor was displaced by graphite in the ends of the rods. Graphite slows neutrons more than water, so the reaction speeded up (see box above). This was the opposite of what the reactor operators expected, since their training had not covered these details. Moreover, the design of the rod reinsertion mechanism meant that they took approximately 30 seconds to drop into place – an eternity in the world of nuclear physics. The absence of the other, disabled safety mechanisms compounded the danger. The power surged and the reactor exploded.

Beyond planning the system to a given risk tolerance, all operators also plan for disaster recovery. Western's view is that 'the key to emergency planning is to understand how to make decisions when things have changed [from routine to extreme]. The plans have to be realistic and simple. You have to practise changing modes.'

For the emergency planning to be effective, the plans must be practised. Holloway reports that 'We have disaster recovery plans. We have [a big exercise] every couple of years. They're a bit cumbersome. The key part is evacuation, and then the medical management of decontamination. Practices for nuclear weapons accidents are more serious, and can involve thousands of people.' Such military exercises aim to limit the consequences of any nuclear weapon accident and reduce the probability of the acquisition of nuclear material by enemies of the state to ALARP, consistent with the overall risk appetite.

This linkage of the civilian and military nuclear establishments illustrates a broader point about risk appetite. Nuclear waste can be (and most often is) rendered unusable and unstealable by mixing it with concrete and setting it in very heavy blocks. In addition, however, weapons-grade material such as plutonium is kept in usable form by the nuclear powers under very high security. This risk, of maintaining potentially stealable stocks of weapons-grade material is taken by conscious choice. Steinberg's point about the association of nuclear power with nuclear weapons is only half the story: it's not just that the public associates them, it's that they are deeply and intimately connected. The ongoing controversy over Iran's nuclear power plans centres on this issue. This connection will continue to be a very real factor in all aspects of the industry, not least in the *thinking, planning* and *doing* in risk management.

SAFETY CULTURE

The most likely cause of an accident is more prosaic. Holloway's opinion is that 'The biggest risk is that people don't follow procedures, as this invalidates all your calculations. For example, in Japan two people were killed when they bypassed safety procedures and created a critical mass of uranium solution in a bucket.'

Consequently, just as in the extractive industries (see Chapter 7), today the nuclear industry puts a massive emphasis on creating a 'safety culture'. One part of this is training. As in flying and drilling, simulators are used intensively. Western says 'We do a lot of [training] work on simulators. They show how a real plant would behave, but it's not absolute veracity.'

Steinberg too emphasizes training. He believes that:

> Our training is the most modern in the world. We have full scope simulators on all sites. The simulators are identical to the control rooms on the sites, down to the colour of the walls. We use a full virtual [computer] model to generate internally consistent [reactor] test scenarios. We also run historical scenarios. We use the simulators to train operators in all modes of reactor operation – start-up, normal operation, shut-down and so on. All operators – who by the way all have engineering degrees, unlike in the West – receive 10 to 14 days' training on the simulator each year.

In addition to training, the other part of creating a safety culture is embedding the value of safety in everyday processes, from top to bottom. 'You see everything through the lens of safety. So much so you tend to forget [that it's there]. Outsiders are shocked by how much safety permeates everything', notes Western.[3]

Another leg of safety culture is the safety audit. Both firms, through independent inspection departments, and regulators regularly review safety in theory and in practice. A further leg is technological. Reactors are built with a 'spider's web' of surveillance and monitoring equipment. Temperature, pressure, flow rates, neutron density and other critical indicators are monitored constantly, as is the functioning of the monitors. If monitors disagree on status, they can 'vote' on what the correct status should be. If something unexpected happens, wherever possible intervention is designed to proceed without power and without manual intervention.

---

[3] Himself included, apparently. He explained, 'I was an environmental campaigner at university. I joined [the nuclear power industry] because I wanted to find out more about nuclear energy. It was more complicated than I thought.'

WAR

However, even with the best self-monitoring monitoring equipment, operating a nuclear reactor is like landing a plane on a windless day in heavy fog. In these conditions, pilots have to rely completely on their instruments for orientation. Similarly, nuclear power plant operators get information only from the control panel. They are cut off (with reason) from the reaction; there is no sensory input at all. They have to infer what's happening from this information, and if something goes wrong they may have very little time to react. At Chernobyl, it was as if the pilots thought that they were flying at a safe altitude when the ground appeared suddenly in the windscreen of the aircraft. Less than 60 seconds after the test started, the reactor exploded.

Steinberg was at the heart of the *doing* after the accident, although fortunately for him, he was not on site at the time:

I had been involved in the construction of the plant, when it was just a clearing in the forest, [but] had been away for three years. At the time of the accident I was deputy chief engineer at another power plant in Russia. I heard about the accident at 7.30 am the same day. The information was not clear – there had been a fire, some deaths. I decided to go to the plant when I realized the true scale of the accident. By the time I arrived [three days later], there were already 200 people in hospital... [including] nearly all the managers and the deputy chief engineer.

It was very emotional. For the first month, there was no time to think or feel anything. The first priority was to protect the staff from radiation. The key was to persuade them that they would survive, that this was routine work. People who believe they're saving their country are ready to die. People who are doing routine work behave normally.

After a week, the situation was new but no longer dangerous. For five or six months, until we had completed the decontamination, it was very unusual. We adapted quickly, like the military when they go to war. We didn't know for months what had happened, as we couldn't look inside the reactor!

Knyshevich also uses the military analogy:

At the time of the accident, we didn't think about radiation. We had to liquidate the accident. When the soldier goes to war, he fights, he doesn't think about being killed. Here [in Slavutich, the new company town built to replace Pripyat] we don't talk about before and after the accident, we talk about before and after the war.

Reihktmann started work at Chernobyl in 1977 after several years as an officer on a nuclear submarine. By the time of the accident he was one of the heads of the operator shifts on reactors 3 and 4. Like Steinberg, with whom he is close, he was intimately involved in the *doing*, the recovery effort. His account offers rare insight into what it's like to manage an ongoing catastrophe:

> Someone came to my flat and said 'Something's happened, you have to go in.' Then another life began. I arrived at the plant at 7.00 am. By 10.00 am the head of the reactor shop was too sick to work. I became the head of the nuclear shop. First I changed the shift patterns to manage radiation doses. Then I appealed to the Communist Party to organize an evacuation. The reply came back that plant management was no longer responsible for Pripyat, the State Commission was in command. Third, I called my wife to tell her to be ready – to the extent that I could without giving away state secrets. I told her to take all our documents, jewellery and winter clothes. By telling her to take winter clothes on a hot day in April, I meant to tell her that she would be gone some time.
>
> The evacuation started at 12 noon on the 27th. There were 1,200 buses altogether. It took less than two hours. I came home from work that night to an empty flat and had a drink. The next day I went to work [at the plant] and every day since then I've worked there.
>
> The liquidation had two stages. In the immediate aftermath we had to put out the fire in reactor 4 and switch off reactors 1, 2 and 3. By mid-May we knew what had happened but not how. Then we had to manage the consequences, basically put the [object] shelter up. The shelter was operational by 13 November.
>
> The most difficult thing was to employ the right people. Few people wanted to work there. Management didn't offer to send people from other reactors. I was ready to employ students and teach them myself. Anyone who was motivated enough to ask, got trained. Working on reactor 4 was safe but difficult psychologically. It was work for real men.

It seems that such macho sentiments are not unusual in the former Soviet Union. Holloway tells a story of a visit there. His host drove a Volvo, a car known in the rest of Europe for its safety features. One such feature was, and is, an annoying pinging alarm that sounds when one of the front-seat passengers has not buckled the safety belt. When the alarm sounded, Holloway looked for his seatbelt, only for his host to pass him a 'seatbelt stub', a contraption consisting only of the head of the seatbelt, designed to fool the alarm. His host smiled and said 'It's not really required.' Holloway countered 'Yes it is. It's required by me.' As he strapped himself in, he thought to himself, if this is how they understand risk, how do they manage a reactor? Tell this story to many Ukrainians

– and others – today and they'll laugh and say 'Why bother? Everyone knows you can just sit on the seatbelt.'

HUBRIS AND HUMILITY

Thinking, planning and *doing* are more closely linked in a nuclear power plant than in most other environments. This is because a nuclear power plant is utterly man-made, unlike most of the other extreme environments in this book.

The first key to risk management in this environment is to exploit this level of control. This starts with *thinking* about an explicit expression of risk tolerance. As Steinberg puts it, you have to decide 'What does it mean, acceptably safe?' In the United Kingdom the nuclear industry, and by implication society in general, works off a tolerance of one chance in 10,000 per year of a fatality. This abstract risk tolerance is then fed into the planning process as a design requirement. Engineers design the plant and write operational procedures, and emergency managers create disaster recovery plans, in such a way that this tolerance is expected to be met. The plant design and procedures and the emergency plans form the basis for *doing*.

Doing in this context means creating an environment where safety is embedded in everyone's actions, all the time. This is difficult since systems that are designed to very high tolerances break down very infrequently. Moreover, most of the time nuclear power plants don't feel very extreme to those who work there. They feel more like a large, comfortable factory: all the dangerous bits are far from view. This apparent absence of risk can induce complacency, leading to accidents.

At the operational level, the foundation of a safety culture is training, both for day-to-day management and for emergencies, and ongoing refinement of designs and procedures based on lessons learnt. This *think–plan–do* process is similar to that used in extractive industries. The main difference is that extractive industries face greater natural hazards. For example, offshore installations are routinely exposed to severe weather, and deep underground there are natural hazards including heat, water and poisonous gases.

However, this is not the end of the process of risk management, because *stuff still happens*. Risk can be managed but not eliminated. The designers of the Chernobyl plant never foresaw that it would end up in the operational state it was brought into prior to the safety test, still less that many of the safety systems would be turned off when it was. Today's designers often express extreme confidence that nothing like Chernobyl could happen with today's reactors. They are probably correct, but who's to say that the next disaster will follow a historical pattern? This kind of 'latent' risk is almost impossible to foresee, even with the best design engineers and emergency planners. The best training in the world cannot create infallible operators.

The best, brightest and best trained are, however, susceptible to hubris – excessive confidence in their own ability. Nuclear power plants are extraordinarily complicated systems, and they and their operators can behave unpredictably. Therefore the second key element of risk management is the acceptance and communication of the limits of certainty: humility to balance the hubris. At one level, this is simply a reflection that our lifespans are too short to come to a judgement about some of the statistics involved. If a component that is used once a day is engineered to a 1 in 1 million standard, the fact that it hasn't failed after 20 years doesn't necessarily prove its reliability. More generally humility means that, in Western's words, 'No one should be fooled that these tools give you the "right answer" – that doesn't exist. Some things you can quantify, the rest is judgement. The real value is in forcing you to think through and understand the system in detail.' While it may be difficult to acknowledge and communicate openly about the risks of a catastrophe, it is imperative.

This applies both externally and internally. Externally, it means an open debate about the risks of alternative power sources. This is difficult, given the general public's historical association of nuclear power with nuclear weapons and general lack of familiarity with the underlying science, but not impossible given current environmental concerns, energy costs, levels of radiation from other sources, and apparent comfort with other applications of science they don't understand. Who hasn't looked at an airliner and thought, how on earth does that thing fly?[4]

Internally, at a minimum it means regular independent audits. It also means enforcing the safety culture through incentives: compensation and promotion must reflect attention to safety issues. If, for example, incentives reward only the production of electricity, then it is unlikely that the reactor will ever be shut down for safety reasons.

Humility also makes denial less likely. If you believe that the impossible might happen, unexpected events won't panic you, and you won't freeze. Unfrozen, you'll be able to contribute to recovery.

---

[4] Western reports that when he went to Chernobyl in 1989 the team took its own radiation monitoring equipment. They got twice the dose in the plane flying from London to Moscow and back than they got in a week in the exclusion zone.

APPLICATION TO BUSINESS

While the consequences of failure are not comparable, the principles of risk management in nuclear plants can transfer to the corporate world. First, most elements of corporate activity are man-made, and as a result most risks are to some extent under corporate control. As in nuclear reactors, this is an argument for articulating a risk appetite, designing systems and procedures around that appetite, and building a risk culture through training, incentives and learning.

Corporate quality management programmes such as GE's Six-Sigma are based on exactly this idea of analysing the source of every risk and managing it to a common standard. In the financial world, there are dozens of models that attempt to match the risk taken as closely as possible with the corporate risk appetite, from credit score cut-offs to value-at-risk limits. At the highest level, the concept of 'economic capital' attempts to pull all the risks of an organization together into one measurement of risk. If this measure is much smaller or larger than the institution's risk-bearing capacity, then there is a misalignment of risk-taking and risk appetite.

The unexpected happens in finance too, though, so the second principle – of humility to counter the hubris – applies too. The best risk management systems, procedures and training will not eliminate risk; indeed they may lead to hubris. It is often difficult to explain to executives that despite their prudent and sensible investments in risk management there is still a non-zero risk of the firm going bust. The world's just like that.

And it is not just the statistically challenged who are difficult to persuade. The Nobel prize-winning economists at Long Term Capital Management were so convinced that their models had every angle covered that they could not conceive of a market scenario where they would blow up – yet blow up they did. They and the Soviet physicists who never considered that their reactor could end up in a state they hadn't designed it to withstand were kindred spirits. Such events just didn't compute.

In addition to doing their best to build systems and processes that reflect institutional risk tolerance, risk managers also need to be humble. They should be honest about the limits of the methods they employ, and they should never uncritically accept model results. This humility will allow them to retain the capacity to process unexpected events, and hence not to panic when they occur.

The aftermath of the Three Mile Island accident demonstrates the necessity of both aspects of risk management to corporations. 'The reactor didn't blow up, but it wiped out the [operating] company and flattened the industry', notes Western. To people, their necessity is demonstrated by the experiences of those who survived Chernobyl and had to bury their friends. Zinienko was sick but survived; his colleagues didn't:

> We paid a high price for our work. One and a half months [after the accident] my white blood cell count was down to zero, so I was sent away to recover. After three months I came back to the plant. In the winter of 1987 I went back to hospital. In 1994 part of my lungs were removed. Six people from my shop died, including my deputy.

We shall continue on this theme of risk management in a man-made life and death environment in the next chapter, where we cover extractive industries.

7

Extraction

Interviewees

Danylo Rymchuk	Head, oil and gas emergency response service, Ukraine
Paul McCormack	Formerly health and safety manager at an Exxon Mobil, Aceh, Indonesia; now safety specialist for Conoco Phillips, Australia
Don Kratzing	Health and safety officer, Roc Oil, Australia
Hugh Brazier	Independent security contractor, UK
John Groom	Head of safety, health and environment, Anglo American plc, UK
Anonymous	Mine supervisor, Xstrata, Australia
Sean McGree	Freelance saturation diver, based in France, works worldwide
John Sinclair	Independent offshore safety specialist, UK based

On 14 October 1913 a massive underground explosion occurred at the Senghenydd mine in Wales. The blast killed everyone below ground, 448 miners. William Fisher, a miner who worked on the rescue effort immediately afterwards, wrote a graphic letter about it to his cousin:

> A month has gone since this terrible calamity occurred; we have recovered 165 bodies so far; and 280 still remain below in that deadly atmosphere. Every possible difficulty faces us; roads blocked here and there by falls of roof, ventilation doors blown down... mining experts from all over the country are here devising ways and means of carrying ventilation in... [and] enabling us to penetrate the workings and snatch away the bodies.
> The 'Dead March', what a nightmare. We draw on leather gloves, lift a body on to a sheet of [strong] cloth, wrap it up, then tie it on a stretcher. 'Off

with it, boys,' and what a journey, even to us, used to pit work. Through the murky gloom dimly lit by the swinging lamps carried by the bearers, broken timbers overhead, cracking with the continual squeeze; stumbling over the rough road with the swinging burdens, slipping on rails, sleepers, rough stones, stepping over small falls; timber, here and there the carcase of a horse stretched across the road, bursted and mortifying [sic]. Climbing big falls, squeezing through small hastily prepared passages, great stones hanging overhead, likely to fall any minute… the stupefying heat and bad air, causing the sweat to pour down one in streams… the sickening stench, rising all the time to the face of the man behind. In one place wading to our knees in water…. Some bodies are heavy, too, our wrists giving out before the two miles are covered.

Now the bottom [of the pit shaft] is reached & the cold air chills to the bone. In the carriage with the burden; the hitcher presses the button, up we go, half a mile of shaft in less than a minute, a rushing and settling. Then across the colliery yard, lit by electricity, through groups of men and women. 'Who is it?' 'Don't know, indeed', on we go. To the mortuary, walls piled with coffins; men come forward, noses and mouths covered; unwrap the body; calling out to a man with a book, 'Moleskin trousers, patch on left knee, nailed boots, piece on right heel,' etc, etc, usually the only means of identification, as faces are unrecognizable.

The pity of it all, that flesh should be so cheap!

Men have collected and used coal and oil for centuries. Initially it was a small-scale activity on the surface, but industrialization dramatically increased the risk. As pits deepened, the risks from collapsing shafts and explosions of methane gas and coal dust increased. In addition, successively larger and deeper pits, more workers, and the introduction of explosives and hazardous machinery all made extraction steadily more risky. In parallel, the progressive exhaustion of ready supplies and rising wages in industrialized countries pushed extraction into higher-risk locations deeper underground, out at sea and in far-off countries – that is, into increasingly extreme environments.

GAS FIRE

In such extreme conditions, accidents can be severe. The experience of Danylo Rymchuk and his team at the Ukrainian oil and gas emergency response service fighting a gas wellhead fire in Paltava, Ukraine, in 2004 provides a good illustration. By the time they arrived at the fire the flame was 40 metres high and generating temperatures of over 300° Celsius. The noise level was 140 decibels – louder than a jet engine, deafening and disorientating. 'Noise is the most difficult part to deal with psychologically', says Rymchuk. The air near the fire was dangerously saturated with gas and contaminated with poisonous hydrogen sulphide. The vibrations were so strong they threatened to unseat fire fighters' helmets. And there was no option to do nothing and wait, as 'A fire will burn for years if we don't put it out.'

The wellhead had leaked, and gas condensate had accumulated and then ignited. The explosion blew the top off the well and the whole upward stream of gas caught fire. Everything that was not metal burnt. Rymchuk's 30-man team devised and executed a four-point plan over five days. First, they removed or destroyed all unnecessary equipment at the wellhead. Second, they created a 'water umbrella' by training several high-pressure water streams on the gas fountain from different angles. The water reduced the temperature of the gas stream and so moved the ignition point higher. This reduced the temperature at and around the wellhead, and created a space for the team to work in. Third, they capped the well. They managed this by improvising an improbable Heath Robinson device to thread cables onto the wellhead base without getting too close. They then used the cables to haul a specialized valve – a blow-out preventer – onto the wellhead. They set the preventer up so that flame flared out of one side while they pumped drilling mud into the other to equalize the pressure in the well shaft. When the pressure equalized, the gas stopped flowing, and the fire went out. Afterwards, a fine mist hung over a battlefield scene: an expanse of water-saturated, deeply churned mud littered with odd metal fragments and machine entrails, surrounding the jarringly intact preventer.

In this context you can understand why 2005 was a hard year for the team. Rymchuk is genuinely upset to report that there were no emergencies all year, only training and compliance and preventive work. This is much more difficult work for men with a large 'appetite for adrenaline', he says.

ACEH

Operating in politically unstable countries adds personal security risk to the physical dangers of extraction. In early 1999 Paul McCormack, currently a safety specialist for Conoco Phillips, was a newly arrived health and safety manager at an Exxon Mobil liquefied natural gas (LNG) installation in Aceh, Indonesia. 'It went from paradise to war zone in a couple of months', he recalls.

He arrived just as the Suharto dictatorship collapsed and the Aceh insurgency reignited. After about a month on the job, there was a (vehicle) hijack attempt. Although he suspected that it might be extortion by the army security detail, McCormack requested assistance from a professional security agency – 'I knew about health and safety, not snipers, bombs or ambushes.' Then a company plane was shot at as it took off. By June that year, a mortar shell had landed in the (unfortified) living area, and then the bus transporting workers from the living area to the work site was strafed.

At that point, McCormack felt that 'Our primary control measure – armed escorted convoys – for our primary risk – workers in transit – wasn't working any more. It wasn't risk management any more, it came down to company values: were we prepared to deal with the statistical certainty that someone would get killed?' Moreover, the expatriate staff on site had signed up for a chance to explore a different part of the world while saving some money and enjoying some warm weather. They hadn't signed up for a war. Towards the end, 'we'd have new people turn up and turn right around and leave'. The site was evacuated in early 2002.

In retrospect, he felt that the 'frog in boiling water syndrome' was at work. 'We knew every day what our line in the sand was, and every day the tide would wash that line away. There was some denial.' He feels, however, that they asked for help at the right time, and they felt in control of the situation from that point forward. The contribution of security professionals was especially important in dealing with the military, in establishing and sticking to benchmarks for threat levels, and in methodically planning for contingencies. For instance, they concluded that the airstrip was too small for the full complement of workers to be flown out in one planeload. This would make emergency evacuation under pressure much more difficult. As a result, they developed a plan for a skeleton workforce that could both run the facility and fit on one plane. The difference with Australia, where McCormack is currently based, is enormous. 'Here the only concern is travel time [from the shore to the rig].'

While the situation in Aceh eventually improved, sometimes mining operations have to adapt to a permanent war footing. In 2005 Andrew Selsky of the Associated Press visited and wrote about El Cerrejon, a giant coal mine in a part of Colombia that was controlled by armed forces opposed to the government. He described a heavily militarized operation, where 10 per cent of the employees are security guards and the coal is transported to the coast by armoured trains.

Sometimes the risk is more prosaic. One time when the Australian oil company Roc Oil was importing equipment into a West African country, customs officers opened up a package to examine the contents – then repacked the explosives and the detonators in the same box, unintentionally risking a massive explosion. 'That made my blood run cold', says Don Kratzing, Roc Oil's health and safety officer.

Sometimes the risk management is also less obvious. Hugh Brazier, a security contractor, has used a range of 'soft' tactics at sites in Colombia, including inoculating children and providing shirts for the local soccer team. Brazier notes, 'The only way you can protect these installations and the people in them in the long term is by getting the local community on side.' Kratzing agrees. 'We can't afford to live in barbed-wire compounds, but we wouldn't want to anyway. If we can't live with the local community, we shouldn't be there in the first place.'

ZERO CASUALTIES

Both Rymchuk and McCormack express the same risk appetite: zero casualties. In principle, so does AngloAmerican, one of the largest mining companies in the world. John Groom, the head of safety, health and environment at Anglo, describes how it operationalizes this risk appetite (see the box):

> Two disaster scenarios that cause me to lose sleep are collapsing tailings dams and pit slopes [the sloping side of an open cast mine]. Even when we've put in place risk control measures, there's still residual risk... [and] these are both potentially catastrophic events. In 2001 in Zambia unusually heavy rain caused the collapse of a pit wall and 10 people were killed; earthquakes are another [source of instability]. To manage the risk we require independent audits and we report these to the Board. If an audit identifies an unacceptable risk of a collapse, we will change the mining operation, closing it if necessary.

(Tailings are the waste products left over from ore extraction. Most tailings are stored as a rock/water slurry. As the solids settle, so some of the water can be recovered, leaving a thick paste behind. The whole storage facility is typically called a 'tailings dam'.)

Groom observes that:

> One challenge with a mine is that the working environment changes every day. It's not like a factory. The mine stope is blasted every day. This means that there are different structures in the rock, different geological features. You need constant awareness of what's going on around you, and the training to recognize important changes.

In such an environment, ALARP can only get you so far. Certainly the safety approach described is much more dynamic than that employed in the nuclear industry, perhaps due to the slow rate of change there.

Safety culture at AngloAmerican

Safety has always been managed, but historically it was not led from the top. Committed leadership and a better understanding of leading indicators are moving us from the old style of reactive management. Our expectation now is 'If it's not safe, don't do it.' This requires a culture change, a change of mindset for all our 190,000 people. Personally, I can't see how you can have any goal other than zero injuries – that would be like trying to come second or third in a race.

In principle, Anglo's safety culture integrates *thinking, planning* and *doing*. 'Our conceptual model for safety is the Bradley curve', a safety assessment model developed at Du Pont.

If you look at accident rates over time, you can have an impact with rules, standards, discipline and even fear – basically management effort. [However] management only has so much effort to apply. To get to the next level [of safety], you need to convince people to take responsibility for their own safety. This means that the workforce has to believe management when we say 'We don't want you to get hurt.' Our policy is to have 'visible, felt leadership'. People must feel that the boss wants them to be safe. The final stage is to get teams of people to look after each other – true synergy.

The progression to a safety culture that is based on teamwork is a challenge. It requires real trust between management, employees, contractors and unions. Historically here at Anglo, there was a huge divide between managers and workers. Our successful operations are those where the divide has been bridged and trust established. Sometimes this is easier in new operations. For example, we have a new zinc mine in Namibia staffed by inexperienced miners and we've lost no days at all.

Given the inherent risks in mining, this is impressive.

We've defined 18 risk categories, of which safety, health and environment are three. HIV is another; the rest are things like reserves, commodity prices and so on. For each of them we identify individual risks, and we classify them based on their likelihood, from certain to unknown, and consequences, from insignificant to catastrophic. Each risk is then plotted on a straightforward four-colour risk matrix: red, orange, yellow, green. Any risk that's not green needs a management plan. Simply put, red means control it, eliminate it or just don't do it; orange means proactively manage it; yellow means reactive management; and green means monitoring only.

Risk control is this environment means building safety into the design and safe behaviour into the operation of a mine: 'You engineer out the short cuts so that the easy way is the safe way. If safe behaviour is built into design, it is not a given that we will have an accident.' Anglo closes the loop between doing and thinking by 'capturing and distributing information on these risks, [through] a group-wide integrated risk management system. It integrates previous systems, and we hope that it will put information back into line managers' hands, rather than staying with experts in head office.'

A supervisor at one of Xstrata's mines in Australia, who wished to remain anonymous, outlined that firm's risk management process underground. For routine maintenance and repair work, personnel use a scorecard methodology. They rate different risk factors, including the proposed solution, and assign the overall task a risk score. If the risk score exceeds a threshold – the risk appetite – the highest-scoring risks have to be mitigated before proceeding.

In his view, the biggest problem in a typical 'mundane' environment is complacency. In an environment where risks appears distant and risk management mere mechanistic form-filling, other incentives dominate. In one mine, the lack of serious injury over a long period created a sense of complacency about safety, which was compounded by a workers' compensation scheme that paid out generously on minor injuries. As a result, the mine recorded large numbers of 'slips, trips and strains… incidents but not accidents'. Short cuts and ad hoc changes to procedure were routine, and the system in place for recording incidents was perceived as pointless. This squares with Groom's observations about new facilities being more fertile ground for implanting a true safety culture.

REPAIR DIVING

Sean McGree is a freelance saturation diver who works on offshore oil and gas rigs. He is at the very sharp end of risk management in this environment: the *doing*. 'Several tasks are potentially fatal, there's no real way round it', he explains:

> Currents and the unpredictable nature of the sea can make situations very dangerous. You have an umbilical connection to the diving bell, bringing you hot water, breathing gas, voice communications and power. Its length is controlled so you can't resurface or become fouled in the ship's propellers. You have one minute of gas from SCUBA cylinders per 10 metres of umbilical distance from the bell for use in the event of an emergency... but if your umbilical were severed in poor visibility, you'd lose heat, light, voice communications and breathing gas, and you might not find the bell again. [Although] there's always one man in reserve in the bell while the others work... basically you'd be on your own.

And very likely end up dead. McGhee continues:

> Everything used on a construction site is used underwater, although it's hydraulically powered, not electrical. Cutting equipment is dangerous, such as oxythermic lances – cutting torches fuelled with pure oxygen. If they [were to] blow up they could knock out your faceplate [and you'd die]. We use high-pressure water jets to remove concrete cladding from pipes and marine growth from structures. If a jet hit your leg, aside from the obvious trauma it would inject sea water right into the cells, basically an amputation.

The other danger is uncontrolled decompression. Divers work deep underwater at high pressure, breathing pressurised helium and oxygen gas mixtures. These gases dissolve into their blood system and tissues. (Hence the term 'saturation diver', as divers' body tissues are saturated with gases at a higher than ambient pressure.) If the diver is then exposed to a rapid pressure change by ascending to the surface, the dissolved gases can come out of solution and can form bubbles in the joints or blood vessels. This causes excruciating pain and embolisms, sometimes death:

> We work in the diving bell. On the ship it locks onto a compression chamber... [which] is kept at the same pressure as the dive depth. We're 'stored' there between dives and for up to a month, decompression times depend on the depth and can take up to eight days.

In a particularly grim twist, McGree recounts how:

> toilets in decompression chambers used to be dangerous. One time in the 1980s a diver pulled the wrong sequence of levers to flush and it turned him inside out. Since then they've changed the layout of the flushing system so you can't flush while you're still sitting down.

Divers rely on redundant systems, detailed planning and high skill levels. 'I enjoy the element of risk, it's part of the job, but I'm not stupid. Everything important – breathing gas and power – is triple redundant' (meaning there are two backups in place). As at Xstrata, and in humanitarian demining operations, 'before each job we... identify the risks inherent in the proposed operation. If the risks are unacceptable to the client or the diving contractor, we recast the operation.' In addition, he adds 'all our tools have dead man switches, so they turn off if you stop applying pressure to them'.

Furthermore, divers are required to practise and train rigorously. For example, when we spoke, McGree had just returned from a training course where '[they] simulated storm conditions using big fans' in a pool. In addition, 'once on every contract we do a [practice] emergency diver and bell recovery... [although] I've never had to rescue anyone.'

> Today most incidents are minor, mostly diver error. There hasn't been a commercial diver death in Europe for several years; the last involved a diver being buried while digging a trench for a pipeline in Holland. Elsewhere in the world safety standards are not as closely regulated. Last year [2005] a couple of divers died off India. They were poisoned by pollutants on the seabed around a drilling rig.

Interestingly, because of the underwater transmission of pressure 'all divers had prior warning of the tsunami in 2004 (from the vessels' radar) – about 30 minutes, just enough to get back to the bell and the ship'.

The other potential source of fatal error is in the diving instructions. If surface operators tell a diver that a gas pipe is not pressurized and instead it's full of gas, then welding becomes explosively dangerous.

In addition to daily risk management, coal and oil facilities have emergency management plans. These are cousins of the multi-level plans used in escalating responses to natural disasters such as earthquakes, floods or wildfires. Says Kratzing:

> Each facility has an emergency response plan. The plan has two elements: an operating plan, which covers local issues such as evacuation; and a corporate emergency support plan, which covers corporate issues such as public relations and funding. Rehearsals of the plan are frequent when the facility is new. The crew is given a sealed envelope with a scenario that they then have to act out.

A universal scenario offshore is helicopters going down at sea: 'The results are inevitably a) people haven't read the emergency response plan and b) there are deficiencies in communications.' In general 'training gives you something to keep your mind off the panic... it's mental armament... you have something to do even as the world is collapsing around you.'

LEGISLATION AND SAFETY CULTURE

It is clear that a great deal of thought goes into safety in extractive industries in developed countries. Onshore in the United Kingdom this is in large part a result of over a century of health and safety legislation – a direct reaction to the Senghenydd mine explosion and similar disasters.

Offshore safety in the United Kingdom experienced a similar legislation-led revolution after the North Sea oil platform Piper Alpha burnt down to the stumps in July 1988, killing 165 people, three-quarters of those on board. The recommendations generated by the public enquiry revolutionized health and safety on offshore platforms.

The recommendations became known as the Cullen Report, after its author, the Scottish judge Lord Cullen. One aspect of the safety regime that the report revolutionized was the introduction of mandatory and comprehensive training and qualifications for offshore installation managers (OIMs). A description of one aspect of this qualification – coping with a simulated emergency – illustrates the sophistication of the overall framework.

John Sinclair is an independent offshore safety specialist. He frequently trains OIMs:

> One requirement to become an OIM is to successfully manage a simulated emergency. The simulation has two parts. The first part is in a mock-up of a rig control room. The mock up has CCTV [closed circuit television] feeds from different parts of the 'rig' and a full fire control panel. The candidate sees warnings from the fire control panel, CCTV footage, and audio inputs such as explosions and intercom messages consistent with a real emergency, such as a fire, a helicopter crash or a tanker collision. Scenarios generally last for 20 to 35 minutes. The longest scenario is a bomb threat.
>
> The second part is on board a live rig (or exceptionally, a practice oil platform, although this misses a lot). The candidate is put into the control room and is shown fake footage and hears fake sound effects and messages, both internal and external.
>
> The reactions of the candidate are judged by a panel of experts, often former nuclear submarine commanders. The judges are especially interested in how the manager reacts during the first hour when only partial information is available and consequently ambiguity is high. How do the candidates piece together and verify the information that they have? What

additional information do they seek? What decisions do they make based on the information to hand?

Unfortunately, risk management in developing countries lags far behind this level of sophistication. For example, almost 6,000 died in Chinese coal mines in 2005; there were over 100 deaths in six separate incidents in one week in July 2006. Indian mines also have much higher accident rates than mines in developed countries. In September 2006, 54 miners died in an explosion in Jharkand.

The point is that there is a choice. Extracting materials from deep underground or underwater is an intrinsically hazardous activity, even more so when the materials are combustible and pressurized, and yet more so when there is physical danger above ground as well. However, mines and oil rigs are ultimately human creations, and thus humans decide how safe they are. With sufficient attention to risk management, the environment can be made tolerably safe, even in the face of natural hazards such as storms.

Since in the past improvements in safety have been imposed on companies rather than driven by them, some scepticism of Anglo's account is appropriate. Indeed, Anglo has many critics. However, the environment, not safety, is the principal subject of the criticism. Accidental deaths at Anglo have declined from 60 in 2000 to 46 in 2005. Anglo converts this to a fatal injury frequency rate (FIFR), the number of deaths per 100 person years. Anglo's FIFR has declined by almost two-thirds from 0.033 in 2000 to 0.012 by mid-2006.

Thinking about risk in this environment, as in an nuclear power plant, means picking an explicit risk appetite, under pressure from government, the media and the public, then *planning* facilities, equipment and procedures so that they function to that level of risk tolerance. The first part of *doing* is enforcing the operating procedures through the safety culture, ideally by leading from the top.

The second part of *doing* is coping with the unexpected. No matter how good your design and procedures, eventually something unexpected will happen. A drill bit might hit an unexpected pocket of high-pressure gas so the well blows up; a government might collapse and your army security detail might morph into armed extortionists; a 1 in 200 year storm might appear on the radar. This is the same point regarding hubris made in the chapter on nuclear power. However, hubris is somewhat less likely in extreme extractive environments. On a North Sea oil rig in a storm, you can't deny the inherent danger you're in, as can be the case sitting in the control room of a nuclear power plant.

The good news is that facilities in a physically hazardous environment, such as the North Sea or Siberia, are usually far from population centres, so in an emergency you can evacuate before solving the problem if you have to. The bad news is that this same distance makes response slower, hence McCormack's point about travel time above. The key then is to adjust the recovery plan to the environment and execute it rigorously, without accepting more risk as the situation deteriorates and implicitly increasing risk appetite in the process.

APPLICATION TO BUSINESS

There are transferable lessons from extreme extractive industries to business. They are similar to those in the last chapter on nuclear power plants. Mines and oil rigs are not natural features of the landscape. They are man-made, as are businesses. Most risks faced by businesses are to some extent under their control. If desired, these risks can be managed by cycling through the *think–plan–do* process: articulate a corporate risk appetite; design operations and procedures to that standard; build a risk culture through rehearsals, training, and incentives; and learn from experience.

The greatest lesson for business from risk management in this environment is to beware of complacency. In the absence of strong leadership, after a period without accidents, standards may slip, and perceptions of risk are gradually reset. To the author, such complacency appears endemic in the financial markets at the time of writing. Defaults in risky assets have been low for an extended period; returns on risky asset classes have been high; volumes of risky assets, and their derivatives such as collateralized debt obligations (CDOs), are growing fast. Managers who counselled caution have been outperformed by those who have chased returns and growth. Risk acceptance standards, such as minimum payment coverage ratios or change of control covenants, have been weakened. All credit instruments – corporate, high-yield, consumer and emerging market – are 'priced for perfection', meaning that any deviation from an optimistic outcome will make them look overpriced. At some point the intrinsic risk of these activities will reappear, accidents will occur, and behaviour will become more risk-sensitive again.

At a slightly more abstract level, this environment illustrates a paradox. If you successfully design a system to prevent certain events, they will indeed occur very infrequently. The absence of events, even if it is known that they are rare and their absence is to be expected, leads to a gradual reduction in the perception of risk. This will in turn lead to an increase in risk appetite and neglect, conscious or unconscious, of risk management policies and procedures. At one level this is a manifestation of what Nobel prize-winner Daniel Kahneman calls the availability heuristic: a cognitive bias that favours recent experience. At another, it becomes a form of moral hazard, as actors are implicitly relying on everyone else to follow the procedures even as they do not. Its consequence, as noted by academic safety specialist James Reason, is that the severity of rare events increases with the time since the last instance. The paradox is that designing a system to reduce the frequency of rare events may end up making their severity worse.

In business environments where there is no physical danger, there is more flexibility here. For example, most trading desks set risk limits so that they are broken frequently, usually about one day in every 20. You couldn't set up a mine so that there was an accident every 20 days. This ensures that the process around managing limit excesses is well-practised. However, it risks desensitizing traders to risk limits. Another concrete example is fire alarms and practice evacuations. If you conduct them too often, there will come a point where no one will respond. As when communicating about risk, there is a sweet spot between frequency and responsiveness.

The last transferable lesson derives from McCormack's experience in Aceh. Even if the risk level changes, keep your risk appetite constant. If the risk rises above your risk appetite, leave. Don't rationalize the change in risk and end up like a boiled frog. The transferable lesson is to stick to your risk limits and standards – otherwise what are they for? If a trader breaches a stop-loss limit, the presumption should be that he or she must close out the position to get back under it. In this close-out process, risk managers should have backing from senior management if the trader escalates. Without this backing, the risk manager is merely a paper tiger who is only able to force traders to sell things they already wanted to sell.

In the next chapter we examine risk management practices when faced with an extreme natural hazard, flooding.

8

Flood

Interviewees

Jesse St Amant	Plaquemines parish emergency services manager, Louisiana, USA
Walter Maestri	Jefferson parish emergency services manager, Louisiana, USA
David Bonner	Flood forecasting specialist, UK Environment Agency
Jay Punia	Chief of flood operations, California Department of Water Resources, USA
Stephen Naylor	Thames Region flood forecasting team leader, UK Environment Agency
Hassan Mashriqui	Professor, Louisiana State University Hurricane Center, USA
Rick Burnett	Flood-fighting specialist, California Department of Water Resources, USA
Gerry Kopp	California Governor's Office of Emergency Services, USA

On Friday 26 August 2005, three days before Hurricane Katrina hit New Orleans, Plaquemines parish emergency services manager Jesse St Amant gave his wife a simple choice: 'Get out or get divorced. We were in constant contact with the weather services', he explains:

> They have five separate models. For Katrina, all five converged on Friday evening. We knew it was going to be bad... it wasn't a case of if but when. I was worried that it wouldn't be a close hit but a direct hit. The models said it would hit 12 miles away plus or minus 50 miles... we knew

from Hurricane Andrew that for a category 3 or above storm, the 20 miles around landfall are total catastrophic destruction. You need to predict that part since the people who live there [before] won't be there [after].

We declared an emergency [evacuation] pre-landfall. At 9.00 am on Saturday morning I was on TV. We achieved 99 per cent evacuation [by the time] the storm hit. I didn't evacuate – as an emergency manager, you 'live and die by the sword' – and neither did the parish president. It was a gamble, but it was a good decision. It was pretty tough until Monday night.

Others also stayed behind. 'Two hundred and forty-two people chose not to evacuate and became S and R [Search and Rescue] victims. We lost four dead, two missing. In this society you have the right to live and die where you want, but one death is too many.' St Amant pauses for a second, then continues. 'Overall, Katrina could have been a lot worse. Anything under 60,000 [dead] was good – there were 1.6 million people in the risk area. If the eye [of the storm] had made landfall 12 miles to the west...' He does not elaborate, but merely states 'We were lucky.'

On the other side of New Orleans, St Amant's peer emergency manager at Jefferson parish, Walter Maestri, also sent his family away on Friday:

I sent [them] to Lafayette. Late Thursday and early Friday the National Hurricane Center communicated to us that this would be a serious storm, with a lot of damage. The structures we have [in Jefferson] are not built to cope with high wind speeds. The only effective response was to evacuate.

Maestri did not call for a mandatory evacuation:

What is mandatory evacuation? What does that mean? Do I put them in jail? I've already evacuated the jail. Our view is 'This is the risk, here are your options, now it's up to you.' For those who stay behind, there are no guarantees [although there is access to] unmanned 'last chance refuges'.

The bottom line? 'Staying behind is stupid.' Maestri, like St Amant, stayed. 'I personally don't evacuate. The job requires that I stay. We stay in the parish emergency operations center, a bunker basically. It's the only structure in the parish that could survive a category five storm.' With a chuckle, he adds:

It's above ground... the first New Orleans emergency management operations center was underground.

We were fortunate. Jefferson parish is the quintessential bedroom suburb, fairly affluent. People have significant resources and they can afford hotels and so on. Those who had the means to evacuate were convinced to do so, and about 90 per cent of the population, 1 million people, evacuated. They knew what a category 5 storm could do. We had very few casualties or fatalities.

At about 6am on Monday 29 August 2005, Hurricane Katrina made landfall 12 miles from New Orleans as a severe category 3 hurricane with winds of about 125 miles per hour. Despite evacuation orders, an estimated 50,000 to 100,000 people were still in the city (as distinct from neighbouring parishes like Jefferson and Plaquemines). By mid-afternoon, several levees had been breached or overtopped. Flood waters poured into the city. Some neighbourhoods ended up 20 feet under water. When the floods receded, they revealed catastrophic damage. Over 1,500 people had died. Insurance losses may exceed $35 billion, the largest in US history by far.[1] New Orleans has lost more than half its population, probably permanently.

A 1 IN 100 YEAR STORM?

Thinking about flood risk is in principle straightforward. You simply pick the frequency of flood that you want to protect yourself against. For example, David Bonner, a flood forecasting specialist at the UK Environment Agency, states the Agency's risk appetite as a 1 in 100 year fluvial (river) flood, a 1 in 200 year coastal flood, and a 1 in 1,000 year flood in London. These are average figures across the full range of terrain; there are local variations. Jay Punia, the chief of flood operations at the California Department of Water Resources, elaborates:

> The level of protection varies depending on land use. Agricultural land might be protected against a 1 in 10 or 1 in 20 year flood, most metropolitan areas are protected to at least 1 in 100 years. We want to move to 1 in 200 year protection, partly as a result of Hurricane Katrina.

New Orleans' levees were designed to protect the city up to and including a category 3 hurricane on the Saffir-Simpson five-point scale. Such storms are defined as winds from 111 to 130 miles per hour and a storm surge of 9 to 12 feet above normal. According to the US National Oceanic and Atmospheric Administration, between 1851 and 2005, 21 category

---

[1] According to the National Weather Service, Hurricane Andrew in 1992 caused insurance losses of $16 billion, equivalent to $26 billion in 2005 dollars.

4 or 5 hurricanes hit the United States, an average of about one every seven years. Five of these storms hit Louisiana. Given that Louisiana's coastline extends for 400 miles, and that a hurricane front is 100 miles wide, this implies that any particular place on the coast has a one in four chance of being hit. An illustrative, unscientific calculation gives $21/154 \times 5/21 \times 1/4 = 105/12,936 = 0.8$ per cent per year chance of a category 4 or 5 storm, about 1 in 100. A 100 year storm.

FLOOD PROTECTION

Planning in flood risk management is then the exercise of converting this risk appetite into credible flood protection defences, plans and policies. The first step is to understand how deep the floods will be across a region under different weather scenarios – 'Who is affected how badly by a hurricane of given force?' in the words of St Amant. This requires detailed scenario modelling combining what has happened with what might happen. St Amant notes grimly, 'Hurricanes have a mind of their own. In New Orleans, we have a lot of experience [with them]… you learn the hard way.'

Stephen Naylor is the regional flood forecasting team leader for the Thames Region at the UK Environment Agency. Part of his responsibility is to create and maintain flood models to support planning. He notes that 'Floods create knock-on effects as tributaries back up. It's like a thrombosis' (a blood clot in an artery). These contagion effects can produce counterintuitive results. For example, flood control features can make flooding worse.

Indeed, some forecasters' models predicted that New Orleans' defences might not withstand a category 3 storm, the stated risk appetite. For example, in 2004 Ivor van Heerden, Mashriqui's colleague at the LSU Hurricane Center, wrote with remarkable prescience that 'recent research reveals that a slow-moving category 3 hurricane, on any number of tracks, could flood New Orleans, levee to levee'. He went on to predict the consequences: 'floodwaters would have a residence time of weeks. The resultant mix of sewage, corpses and chemicals in these standing flood waters would set the stage for massive disease outbreaks and prolonged chemical exposure.' Some of these predictions were borne out by events, others were not. The flood waters took five weeks to pump out. There was no outbreak of disease (cholera was feared). Toxic arsenic, lead and diesel fuel contaminants persist in several locations at high, some say unsafe, levels.

Flood modelling

Flood models such as the model used by Naylor at the UK Environment Agency or Mashriqui at LSU are composite models combining models of each of the components of a flood: rain, wind, waves, tide and atmospheric pressure. They are very rich, drawing on deep historical datasets and employing sophisticated simulation engines.

'We have predictive hydrodynamic models for fluvial floods [in the Thames watershed]. Our models are calibrated against actual rainfall data from previous events', says Naylor. 'They include full survey details of the cross-section of the river all along its entire length, a digital terrain model, a hydraulic model... and flood defences', actual and hypothetical. He continues:

> We input rainfall data, then model the depth of flooding at each of about 4,000 nodes [points] in the river. Each node is a stretch of 50 to 100 metres or a structure. [We overlay the results] on maps and property data to create loss distributions. The results are non-linear: a low level of flooding may not cause much damage, but as soon as the water gets to the height of electrical sockets, it gets serious.

Professor Hassan Mashriqui at Louisiana State University's (LSU) Hurricane Center takes the output of hurricane models as his input. He modelled Hurricane Katrina's path through New Orleans, and found that:

> Poorly designed man-made features can aggravate the storm surge. In New Orleans the city flooded from the east side through three man-made canals, [including] the Mississippi river gulf outlet [MRGO], a canal that runs from south-east to north-west. It carries lots of water during a storm surge.

According to Mashriqui, the MRGO was a 'Trojan Horse in the flood defences'. Acting like a funnel, it amplified and accelerated the storm surge even as it directed it towards the city's heart. This amplified surge contributed significantly to levee overtopping and collapse. Amazingly, 'the builders never looked at storm surge, only the commercial basis'. (And this too was suspect. The predicted traffic never materialized.)

Flood models also build in long-term drift in important variables. For example, UK tidal models build in a 6 millimetre rise in sea level per year. 'Three millimetres of this is south-east England tipping [geologically],' says Naylor, 'and three millimetres is global warming.' There is considerable uncertainty about this last variable: in 2006 scientists working for the Environment Agency raised the possibility that a second Thames flood barrier might be required to combat the effects of climate change. The integration of climate change into flood models will be the direction of travel for flood models for the years to come.

MODELS IN THE COMMUNITY

Flood simulation models sketch the contours of losses under different flood scenarios. These contours identify, for example, which hospitals, police stations, power plants and other essential facilities would be under water at the chosen risk appetite. This information is of more than academic interest to the affected communities. Modellers thus share it with them. In most cases, communities then create flood management plans based on this information and their own priorities. For example, in California, Punia explains, 'each community develops its own flood contingency plan. We provide them with simulations of area flood footprint, depth, flow and timings as input.'

Many communities ask for flood protection based on the model output. Punia oversees 1,600 miles of levees in central California. In the Netherlands an extensive network of dykes protects the 27 per cent of the country that lies below sea level. In London, there is the Thames flood barrier. It was designed as part of a national flood defence programme after a massive storm surge caused severe flooding and 307 deaths in 1953.[2]

Naylor elaborates:

The Thames Tidal Flood Barrier opened in 1984. It will provide protection up to 1 in 1,000 year standard until 2030, even with climate change. It can also close at low tide to create a reservoir to offset fluvial floods. We've had years when we've used it 20 times, and years when we haven't used it at all. In 2005 we used it six times.

---

[2] Because of the same surge 1,783 people died in the Netherlands. Dutch flood defences are designed to a 1 in 4,000 to 1 in 1,000 year standard, according to Risk Management Solutions (RMS).

On average the barrier has been closed against tidal surges two and a half times per year since completion. Recent years have been above this level, however. In 2001, the barrier closed 11 times; in 2003, eight times. There is disagreement over whether the flood barrier provides the appropriate level of protection. One source, who wished to remain anonymous, described it ominously as 'a Maginot Line'. The implication is that it provides a false sense of security.

More generally, Naylor continues:

> Each catchment area must have a flood management strategy. There is a scoring system for flood defence budget allocation based on the probability, impact and required standard [of defence]. Any project that is over the threshold can be considered. We can introduce flood defences and see what the difference in damage would be. We don't look at each part of the river in isolation, [as] the solution may be upstream.

Sometimes flood defences may not be worth it. Bonner notes that 'if it costs hundreds of millions [of pounds] to protect a village, sometimes we have to say sorry'. Equally, certain flood risks may never be identified. For example, in New Orleans it appears that few thought about the practice of storing original documents in basements. The flood destroyed many medical and financial records as a result, paralysing some recovery activities.

LIMITING DEVELOPMENT IN FLOOD PLAINS

There are alternatives to building static flood defences. One is controlling development in areas prone to flooding. Naylor explains that:

> We are actively trying to reduce development in the flood plain. We try to talk to developers before they apply for planning permission. We give them lots of detailed information – we're trying to influence and educate. In general they're pretty responsive. [In addition] we are a statutory consultee on development projects in the floodplain or where they impinge upon a watercourse. We can object to projects, and impose conditions such as flood relief tunnels and minimum heights for access roads. The local council has the final say on approval but they have to have good reasons not to accept our conditions.

If developers and counsellors don't listen, insurance companies may. Bonner's department has 'done a lot of work with insurers in the past few years. After [the floods in] 2000 they stripped lots of coverage.' This seems to have had some effect. In cases where coverage is still provided, prices have risen. In addition, insurers have voiced concern about the UK government's plan to relieve the housing shortage in the south-east of the country through a massive construction effort in the 'Thames Gateway' region.

The most extreme plan is to turn the clock back. Naylor observes that:

> We've had a wider, more strategic remit in the past 10 to 15 years. Now we're also charged with improving [wildlife] habitats and so on. In some cases the natural environment can provide flood defence and habitat and recreation. Sometimes we return things to their natural state – put some meanders back into a river for example. In some cases we have knocked down houses and returned an area to nature.

Mashriqui agrees. 'Natural barriers – forests, swamps, wetlands – can mitigate natural events. All over Asia, for example – in Japan, Fiji, Papua New Guinea, Bangladesh – [people] are regenerating mangrove forests as [coastal] flood protection.' Other flood-prone river basins are reducing their flood risk by reforesting upstream watersheds, some of which had been denuded by forest fires.

In addition to allowing the planning of flood defences, both natural and man-made, information sharing builds credibility. Maestri attributes part of the successful evacuation of Jefferson parish to this effect:

> First you analyse the risk, understand it. Then you communicate it to your constituency. To start with you're only talking possibilities, but over time the band narrows. If you present it factually, people will work with you. We used every mechanism available [to communicate]: lectures, presentations, videos of computer simulation output, our website. Nobody in our community didn't understand the risk. People could look up the results for their own address, see the impact. It takes that kind of factual information to effect a response.

Once the flood defences are in place, the next stage of planning is to develop contingency plans. In California, Punia explains: 'based on our simulations of flood footprint… each community develops its own flood contingency plan'. In London, 'We are also involved in emergency response', explains Naylor:

> We are a category one responder, in the same league as the blue light services [fire, police and ambulance] under the Civil Contingency Act.

We work closely with local authorities and the emergency services as part of the resilience forums. We identify evacuation sites... [and] conduct rehearsals.

Contingency plans extend both horizontally and vertically with the size of the flood. They stretch horizontally, in that when a flood is too big for a community to cope, neighbouring communities provide assistance if they can. They go vertically, in that the next higher level of government will also provide assistance. In a Federal country like the United States, there is a strict sequence of escalation from municipal to county to state to Federal agencies. Each step in the escalation process is clearly defined so that there is no confusion in a crisis – at least in theory. In the case of Katrina, this escalation process failed completely for several days while various local, state and federal agencies argued over turf and technicalities.

RISING WATERS

And then we get to *doing*. Large-scale floods differ from other extreme events in that they are not sudden. You can track the storm by satellite and watch the rain falling; telemetric sensors detect the swelling of rivers. Perhaps this explains the strangely compelling experience of watching the Weather Channel. In addition, floods can only occur at the interface of water and land. You know which neighbourhoods are going to be affected, the only question is how badly.

Bonner was the incident commander at major flood in Worthing in the United Kingdom in 2003. 'More rain fell in one night than [had fallen on a single night] for the previous 300 or 400 years.' Using the Agency's flood models, Bonner was able to give the community a final flood evacuation warning three hours in advance. 'The key is to give warnings as early as possible.' However, he notes, 'It's a fine balance. You can't give warnings before the rain has fallen. How confident do you have to be to issue an evacuation order?' The answer is that in an uncertain world, as a risk manager you'll err on the side of caution and hence get it wrong more often than you get it right. A risk manager needs a thick skin in order to be able to take the criticism that follows such a 'wrong', yet conservative, call.

Rick Burnett is a flood-fighting specialist in California. With 30 years of experience as a first responder, including time as a wildfire fighter, he has often been the man on the front line:

In 1997 we had one of the worst high-water events in California history. It was late December, just after Christmas. We were alerted by the National Weather Service that a series of storms was lining up in the Pacific. We began to organize between Christmas and New Year's – we sent people out to areas of historical concern, mainly along the Sacramento and America rivers. They touched base with the local agencies, trying to get ready. There wasn't much to do preventatively at this stage.

On the 31st I was in the Chico area. [Although] the local stream was overtopping, I didn't have a feeling of great doom approaching. The storm broke on New Year's Eve. By 0200 on 1 January we started getting calls. It took a few days for the Sacramento River system to overtop, but we knew it was going to. It was a solid month of flood fighting.

The previous big flood was in 1986. I was a crew supervisor. Sometimes I jumped into levee breaches to lay sandbags myself. It was exciting, exhilarating. Sometimes we know that an area will be inundated, it's just a question of what's the least bad option. We had a report from a town that the levees were hours away from a breach. The locals asked us to save the newly built library. We sandbagged it. It was the only structure that was saved. Ultimately it's not up to us, it's up to nature.

In a neat summary of the difference between *doing* and *planning*, Burnett notes that:

Flood management is not the same as flood control. Flood management is an emergency response, a damage mitigation exercise; flood control is a managed effort prior to flooding.

Only a quarter to a half of the information you need is available at the centre. The initial responder conducts an assessment from the ground or air, then starts the organization of the response. You need to have the right people at the right places at the right times. We don't really take any specialized equipment with us: rain gear, flotation devices, shovels and burlap bags [used for sand bags]. Usually by the time you get heavy equipment [such as bulldozers], the flood's over.

Burnett's experience is one part of the *doing* – local intervention when floods overcome local defences. Since floods can affect large areas and resources are always limited, this intervention has to be prioritized and directed at the greatest threats. Gerry Kopp of the California Governor's Office of Emergency Services (OES) coordinates the state's flood response from the top:

It's not a lot different from conducting an orchestra. The OES is a broker of information and resources across the state. Like the rest of the state bodies, we use the Standard Emergency Management System [SEMS; see Chapter 9 on earthquakes]. We also obtain federal resources if they are required.

Punia is also part of this system, and plays a key role in managing the process of escalation:

> We are co-located in the joint operations center with the National Weather Service, the California-Nevada River Forecast Center, and organizations covering the operators of dams and reservoirs. During flood season we meet every day at 10 am to discuss threats and strategy given the current situation and the three-day forecast. If there is a risk of overtopping, local agencies implement their contingency plans – a graded response, in accordance with the expected severity. If there is a breach, we coordinate the response between different levels of government. California has flood engineers and flood fight specialists [such as Burnett] on staff and they are dispatched to floods as required.
>
> We cannot completely eliminate flood risk. We can manage it through reservoirs, planning, forecasting, and building. We are trying to make sure that we are never in the situation of New Orleans after Katrina; that we are prepared and have adequate resources to hand. It looks like the coordination between local, state and federal government didn't work well.

SUMMARY

What then are the keys to risk management in flooding? First, when *thinking* about risk, be honest about your risk appetite. It is tempting to announce a conservative risk appetite, then cut corners when implementing the expensive measures necessary. The temptation exists because, by definition, a low risk appetite implies protection against all but the rarest events, so the odds of being found out cutting corners are low. Although flood protection and evacuation plans are rarely tested, it is essential to fund them properly – or simply tell the truth and say that the risk appetite is in fact higher than previously stated.

This applies to risk managers at all levels. Those managing the levees need to make sure they get funding for enhancements and maintenance. Those managing the response of individual companies (or households) need to avoid complacency and its close relative, moral hazard. Rather than assuming that it won't happen, or that even if it did, someone else – 'the authorities' or whoever – would take care of it, risk managers need to have a plan that will withstand extreme circumstances. In St Amant's words, 'People who live in [flood zones] must accept responsibility. Part of their responsibility is to have a plan.'

Sadly in New Orleans there were indications over several years that the flood defences might be breached in a strong category 3 storm like Katrina, yet a budget for strengthening the levees was repeatedly refused by governments from both political parties. Moreover, the contingency plan largely failed to operate – pump operators were sent home, emergency responders were unavailable, evacuation buses were submerged, residents were abandoned, federal and state aid were delayed – for reasons that are still unclear but appear to be simply poor management. Maestri laments that 'We made it known to federal and state officials that the resources weren't there. The resources did not come; the plan wasn't implemented.' This recalls the apparent lack of contingency planning by the Pakistani government prior to the earthquake there in 2005 (see Chapter 9).

Second, in contrast with epidemics or terrorist attacks for example, floods are predictable in space, time and intensity. It is possible to estimate with reasonable confidence where, when and how severely floods will occur under certain conditions. Consequently you can subject *planning* to disciplined cost–benefit analysis. If the cost of the flood protection exceeds the cost of the property to be protected, then it's not worth it.

Another consequence of the predictability of floods is that if plans are credible, much of the *doing* can be focused on preventative evacuation beforehand rather than search and rescue afterwards. Successful evacuation requires openness, credibility and a thick skin. As we saw earlier, Maestri is a fanatical communicator, yet he jokes, 'I'd been preaching the risk of catastrophe for a decade. I was known as Dr Doom.' Without humour, he goes on, 'I hate to say that I told them so; I'm sorry I was right.'

If you choose a low risk tolerance, since forecasts are uncertain, it is inevitable that you will be wrong more often than right when calling for an evacuation. You will be cast as Cassandra. Keeping quiet, or worse still pretending everything is fine, then being hit 'unexpectedly' by a storm are alternatives, but they are not risk management. St Amant describes the pressures:

> It's not pleasant to know that what is here today may not be here tomorrow... and who. Each evacuation costs Conoco-Phillips millions of dollars to shut down and start up again. You hope you've done the best that you could. For Hurricane Lilly [in 2002], we didn't evacuate, and when it made landfall I had serious second thoughts.

APPLICATION TO BUSINESS

These lessons are applicable in business. Most obviously, if your business is situated in a flood zone, you should adopt exactly the same approach as described above: find out what the consequences of floods up to your firm's risk appetite would be, plan appropriately, and execute the plan when a storm above your tolerance is coming your way.

There are also applications at a more abstract level. A common cause of trouble at financial institutions is the 'rogue trader'. Management announce that they are shocked – shocked! – to have discovered that an employee has run up vast losses. What is often absent from the announcement is the crucial information that said employee was one of the best revenue generators at the firm in recent times. This was certainly true at Barings prior to its disappearance, UBS prior to the takeover by SBC, and Kidder Peabody prior to its sale by GE. Great rewards, such as trading profits, rarely come without great risks. If you accept the great rewards without inquiring about the underlying great risks – or you inquire but ignore or bury the results, as in the risk management function at Enron – then you have just increased your risk appetite. Your institution is no longer as safe as your bondholders, depositors, shareholders, regulators and employees think it is.

A related phenomenon is to establish risk limits and then ignore them. For example, on trading desks it is standard practice to define a 'stop-loss' limit, meaning that if accumulated losses reach a certain limit, the underlying positions must be sold and the loss realized. This is akin to ordering an evacuation if expected damages exceed a certain threshold.

This simple concept is surprisingly hard to stick to in practice. Traders who don't recover from a large loss tend to move on and disappear from institutional memory. Traders who recover and stay with the institution remind you incessantly of the time you enforced a stop-loss and 'cost' them (and the institution) millions. The cumulative effect is to make limits negotiable where negotiating strength is proportional to profitability. Since high profits usually follow high risk, this results in a particularly dysfunctional dynamic where those most likely to make large losses get most leeway with respect to limits. Limits need to be applied consistently, otherwise the institution's risk appetite is meaningless. Commercial risk managers who are dishonest about their risk appetite risk their own versions of the levees collapsing during Hurricane Katrina. A corollary of this is that risk managers need to have a thick skin, just like 'Dr Doom' Walter Maestri.

Being honest about your risk appetite also applies in determining the appropriate level of insurance and contingency planning. Planning for and insuring against very rare events seems like a waste until they happen. Rational risk management requires working to the stated risk appetite across the board, and paying what is required to achieve that risk appetite – or changing the risk appetite, openly.

One important difference is that risks in business are not usually predictable. Indeed most firms operate in markets that change rapidly and continuously under the pressure of competition. A new competitor may emerge unexpectedly, as Sony found out when Apple and Microsoft entered the portable music and gaming markets respectively; a new technology may appear and demolish your business model, as voice-over-internet telephony appears to be doing to conventional fixed-line telephony. Cost–benefit analyses have to cope with fewer certainties and more intangibles than in flood planning. Few businesses are built to withstand true 1 in 100 year storms. Indeed, very few businesses are 100 years old.

In the next chapter we explore risk management for another natural disaster, earthquakes. Unlike floods, earthquakes occur without warning.

9

Earthquake

Interviewees

Maurice McQuillan	Emergency programme officer, Trocaire, Ireland
Anonymous	Consultant surgeon, volunteer responder to the Pakistan earthquake, UK
John Rowden	Risk mitigation officer, California Governor's Office of Emergency Services, USA
Hiroaki Ubukawa	Manager, Oyo-RMS, Japan

In 1906, a catastrophic earthquake struck San Francisco, California. One Charles B Sedgwick witnessed the results and recorded his impressions.

Buildings by the dozen were half down; great pillars, copings, cornices and ornamentations had been wrenched from the mightiest structures and dashed to the ground in fragments; the huge store-windows had been shattered and costly displays of goods were so much litter on the floors. The sidewalks and roadway were covered with fallen stones, wooden signs and the wreckage of brick walls, the [street] car tracks were twisted, the roadbed here fallen, there lifted, and everything on every hand was either broken, twisted, bent or hideously out of place... the colossal City Hall, the principal edifice of the town, was a hopeless, pitiful wreck; its mighty walls rent; its once beautiful rotunda a great gaping wound; its huge dome supported by nothing but a gaunt skeleton of empty framework. In the side streets the havoc was as bad; in places vastly worse... whole floors had been broken up, stairways had collapsed, marble facings torn away.

And in the rear of this, south of Market Street, a great sea of flame was steadily rolling forward with a dull hungry roar, relieved only by the still louder roar of failing buildings at frequent intervals, and thunderous ear-splitting explosions when dynamite was used in the vain effort to check the fiery advance.

The US Geological Service (USGS) estimates that the earthquake registered 7.8 on the Richter scale[1], and caused about 3,000 deaths and $10 billion (in current values) of damage. Were a similar quake to recur, the California Geological Survey estimates that it would cause over $50 billion in damage.

Sedgwick's description gives an idea of the sheer destructive power of a severe earthquake. Describing the immediate aftermath of the 2005 earthquake in Pakistan and Kashmir, Shaista Aziz of Oxfam captures the human impact.

> The smell of death hangs thick in the air. Everywhere you look there are collapsed houses and buildings; the odd personal belonging here and there scattered amongst the debris. Pakistani Kashmiri women wait for relief aid to turn up at camp. One of the women talked to me at length about how she had lost her two children when her house came crashing down over her head. She said she had managed to survive because it was God's will and she had been chosen to stay alive. I asked where she was living now and she pointed to a tree in the park and told me that she slept under the tree and had nothing, no blanket, no money and no food. It was at this point that I noticed her bulging belly that looked out of place on her fragile frame and I realized that she was pregnant.[2]

The earthquake registered 7.6 in magnitude. The official death toll, as at the end of 2005, was just under 75,000.

In no other extreme environment does such destruction and human loss occur so suddenly. Equally because the destruction is sudden, rescue and recovery efforts can – indeed must – begin almost immediately.

DISASTER IN BAM

In December 2003, a severe earthquake flattened the town of Bam in Iran. Help arrived fast, according to the International Committee of the Red Cross (ICRC):

> Two hours after the quake, the first Iranian Red Crescent teams arrived… [they] saved 157 lives with just 10 sniffer dogs. Neighbours saved hundreds more. Around 10,000 seriously injured people were evacuated. [Almost immediately] Iranian authorities launched an appeal for international aid and waived visa requirements for foreign aid workers – unprecedented

---

[1] The magnitude of an earthquake is a measure of the total energy released. A magnitude of over 7 is a major earthquake.

[2] Source: bbc.co.uk.

decisions. In total, 1,800 aid workers arrived from 44 countries. [They] found 22 people alive.

Maurice McQuillan, emergency programme officer with Trocaire, the Irish Catholic Relief and Development Agency, was one of those foreign aid workers:

I arrived in Tehran about a week afterwards. After spending the night in the airport, I took a flight to Kerman, about 100 kilometres from Bam. I had been in touch with the Turkish Blue Crescent and they sent a car for me. It was early evening when we got to Bam, just before the sun went down. From about 25 kilometres out, you could see the damage. In the outlying villages it was just cracks in mud-brick walls. It got progressively worse – complete devastation – as you got closer. The city itself had just fallen down – almost every building had collapsed – as if a small city like Galway just fell over. People said afterwards it was like a massive wave under your house; seismologists said that the epicentre was right under the city, and the ground elevated up to 5 metres. Even a well-constructed house wouldn't survive ground movements over a couple of metres. In addition, houses in Bam typically had very heavy roofs. Basically, if you were caught inside when it started, you had one minute to get out or you were dead. When I first arrived, people were talking about casualties of 10,000, 15,000, 20,000.

An estimated 27,000 people died in Bam in the end.
McQuillan confirms the ICRC's observation that early assistance is the most valuable:

By the time I arrived there were few people being dug out. I remember being very busy trying to organize food and shelter for the survivors, working 16 to 18 hours a day at the one hotel still standing, and having sixteen things to do at the end of the day, a list of people I hadn't met... and running out of the hotel in the middle of the night with my sleeping bag during aftershocks.

There was no time to process the scale of the disaster. However, man-made violence, such as I've seen in Northern Uganda, is tragic, much more upsetting. It's the worst place in the world... the commanders these days are those who were kidnapped and brutalised 10, 15 years ago... they don't know anything else [but brutality].

COORDINATION PROBLEMS

Earthquakes are not man-made disasters, but without an appropriate search and rescue response the damage can be much worse. A consultant surgeon, who agreed to an interview on condition of anonymity, saw the devastation caused by the earthquake in Pakistan on television and decided to do something about it. He organized a team of colleagues and equipment, and arrived in Pakistan three weeks after the earthquake. He was shocked by the lack of organization:

> At the airport there was aid everywhere – tents, helicopters, food. We went… to the Al-Shiffa hospital in Rawalpindi. It was one young child after another, mostly crush wounds. Gruesome. Some kids were alone; some didn't even know where they were from. There was a TV crew in the operating theatre. We had no idea who they were, only that they were Pakistani. The hospital was completely disorganized, there were patients in the corridors, everywhere. [There was no patient information, so] we started to take names, and to try to combine names, pictures and X-rays into a database.
>
> After a while our beds filled up. There was nowhere to discharge patients to, nowhere for them to go, so we couldn't do any more operations. It was the same in the other hospitals: one patient per bed, 100 per cent occupancy.
>
> After a couple of days we were shown the devastation. We only got an hour out of Rawalpindi – two to three hours from the epicentre – but all you saw was rubble. Any time you got some height, you saw rubble all around, half-collapsed buildings, twisted cables, people's possessions. There were tents all along the roadway.
>
> We looked in on a hospital in a big tent encampment. There was no coordination… no centralized control. For example, no one kept track of dressings, so no one knew what was under the plaster; there were 250 Cuban [doctors] on the front line without a translator. Everyone was doing their own thing.

The chaos affected him and his team deeply. They concluded that the disorganization would continue. 'We did our best, we could do no more. We treated those who would survive the winter.' Given the likely absence of assistance, they felt that 'sometimes it would be kinder to let someone die than to give them treatment but no hope'.

STRONG STRUCTURES, RAPID RESPONSE

The preceding accounts demonstrate the two key elements of earthquake risk management: reinforce structures before the event, and respond rapidly afterwards. The former is more important than the latter. While rescuers saved hundreds of lives at Bam, tens of thousands died. The Northridge earthquake in California in 1994 was about the same strength as that in Bam, and 100 times fewer people died. For earthquakes, building stronger houses is more effective at reducing risk than searching for survivors.

Thinking about earthquake risk is in principle straightforward, as for floods. Earthquakes occur where the edges of the plates that comprise the earth's surface meet and scrape against each other. Geological researchers, such as those at the California and US Geological Surveys, monitor and analyse these 'fault lines' continuously. Earthquakes occur frequently, so they are able to build detailed 'shakemaps' for each fault line. The maps show estimated earthquake frequency and severity at each point on each fault. By matching the impact to engineering assessments of buildings and other structures, risk managers can estimate the damage in their area for any given size of earthquake. To set a risk appetite, they pick a level of severity that they, their company or their community can tolerate and afford. Since severe earthquakes are rare, picking a severity implies a frequency and vice versa. The frequency and severity together are the risk appetite.

This risk appetite is then embedded in the *planning* process. This happens in two ways. One way is to ensure that buildings in general and emergency service facilities in particular won't collapse. This can be achieved through specific building or reinforcement programmes, or through legislation. For example, in California there are at least 12 major pieces of legislation on earthquake survivability. Dams, bridges, marine oil terminals, schools, hospitals, fire and police stations, and emergency operations facilities must be constructed and operated so that they can function after a 'major' earthquake. Additional legislation requires the operators of multiplicative hazards – those whose failure in an earthquake would turn a disaster into a catastrophe – such as nuclear power plants and refineries to ensure the survivability of their facilities. All new buildings are built to be earthquake-resistant. In some cases existing buildings must be reinforced, or even demolished and rebuilt.

In these laws, a major earthquake is defined as over 7 on the Richter scale. This then is California's risk appetite for earthquakes. Earthquakes in this range are expected to occur every two to three years. This would include not only the two most recent major earthquakes, in Loma Prieta in 1989 and in Northridge in 1994, but also the 1906 San Francisco earthquake.

CONTINGENCY PLANNING AND SEMS

The other way to *plan* for earthquake risk is to create a contingency plan. The risk appetite informs this plan as well. The plan ensures that when an earthquake hits, the medical treatment, evacuation, public order and fire-fighting processes all continue to function. The level of functioning should be sufficient to limit damage to the stated risk appetite. Unlike flooding, there is no advance warning from an earthquake, so pre-emptive evacuation is not possible.

John Rowden is the risk mitigation officer for the California Governor's Office of Emergency Services (OES). Like many Californians, he has been up close and personal with an earthquake. He was in Candlestick Park baseball stadium during the Loma Prieta earthquake in 1989. Driving home afterwards, he recalls, 'It was eerie, what you'd imagine the end of the world would be like – no lights, no radio, nothing.'

Rowden plays a major role in contingency planning for earthquakes and other major disasters. The core of California's planning is SEMS, the Standard Emergency Management System (see box). '[SEMS] is a bottom-up approach based on the principles that response starts locally, surrounding communities will provide mutual aid, and one person should be in charge of an incident.' Rowden ensures that local emergency response plans are consistent and SEMS-compatible.

California's Standard Emergency Management System (SEMS)

SEMS got started after severe fires in Oakland in 1989–90 revealed weaknesses in emergency response – and 'burnt down a state senator's home', a cynical observer adds. It standardizes incident management structure, roles, responsibilities, terminology, workflow and data capture. Its foundation is a legal framework (the Master Mutual Aid Agreement, MMAA) that defines the conditions in which communities will help each other in emergencies.

All incident responses have the same structure. The structure consists of five functions: management, covering liaison, public information and safety; operations, with responsibility for fire and rescue, law enforcement, medical and health, shelter, construction, utilities, hazardous material handling and dispensation of assistance; planning, which deals with status reporting, mobilization, planning and expert technical advice; finance, processing time and expense and compensation claims; and logistics, taking care of communications, transport, personnel, procurement, facilities and resource tracking.

SEMS also standardizes the scope of the incident and the response – state, region, operational area (county), local and field – and the seniority of the management required – director, section, branch, group and unit. In general, large incidents have more people in each function and more senior people in charge, and small incidents have fewer of each.

In addition, SEMS provides standard, interoperable information management and satellite communication systems and a framework for training. Every county has a SEMS-trained emergency manager who works with the state emergency management department.

If it is sufficiently rehearsed, the beauty of a standardized response like SEMS is twofold. First, at every incident every participant from every agency knows what is being discussed, what is going to happen, who is going to do it and how, and who will foot the bill – in theory at least. Second, when these standard procedures are combined with local plans and practitioners, emergency response can continue without central orchestration after an earthquake even if individual units are cut off. Each local unit functions independently and arrays its own resources against its local priorities. As contact is re-established, the state-wide organization regroups and reassembles itself. The Department of Homeland Security has adopted SEMS as its model. Rowden notes that the system 'is robust, although he adds that 'we haven't really been tested... Loma Prieta and Northridge weren't that severe'.

Prior to an earthquake, *doing* means enforcing the law, practising the contingency plan and communicating the risks to the public. Enforcement is the province of state and municipal building inspectors. They ensure that new and retrofitted structures comply with regulations.

Rowden coordinates regular contingency plan rehearsals for all hazards faced by Californians:

> So far this year [by November 2005], we've had two state-wide disaster rehearsals. The last one simulated multiple terrorist attacks and involved 3,000 people across multiple locations. It went OK, as expected: the system is robust at a micro-level as we've got lots of trained people in place.

This is a remarkable statement. Rowden was the only risk manager interviewed for this book who expressed this level of satisfaction with his or her rehearsal experience.

Rowden is also actively involved in communication with the public:

> Emergency managers in California are very aware that the citizenry must be involved, simply because of the frequency of disasters. Californians

are aware of hazards – the First Lady's in the process of publicizing a preparedness campaign – but have a tendency to ignore them. There is an underlying confidence in the government's ability to respond.

However, Rowden believes that significant moral hazard is limited in practice by the sheer frequency of events. From 1953 to 2006, the Federal Emergency Management Agency (FEMA) records that on average California declared just over one major disaster every year, with two declared in each of 2004, 2005 and 2006.

After an earthquake, *doing* means getting emergency services in to treat the injured, evacuating survivors, clearing up and rebuilding. In the first instance this means ensuring that emergency services facilities and staff survive the earthquake. This can go beyond structural reinforcement. For example, some fire engine garage doors are seismically activated. If an earthquake hits, the doors open automatically and the fire engines are not trapped inside. Cunning.

In addition California has eight specialized Urban Search and Rescue teams (USAR) based in fire departments throughout the state. The teams are ready to respond to any hazard. Each team has two units of 28 members, providing cover round the clock. Each unit includes individuals with search, rescue, medical and technical skills; is self-contained with food, water, equipment and tools; and is ready for deployment in less than six hours. Their role is to locate, extract and stabilize victims. Similar units are maintained by most large aid agencies, and by many cities, states and countries in earthquake zones. They are mobilized globally and dispatched to earthquakes as required, as noted above in Bam.

McQuillan notes that:

> The first few days are about search and rescue. Local resources that arrive in the first 12 hours can save the most people – although on CNN you see the teams from Switzerland and Australia, by the time they've arrived there are fewer rescue opportunities. After the initial search and rescue effort the next priority is food and shelter and the medical and health needs of the survivors.

Emergency responders use 'shakemaps' to decide where to focus their efforts. In the tracks of the search and rescue teams follow teams to clear debris, repair essential services, organize evacuation where possible and food and accommodation where necessary.

While this is expensive, 'cost is not an issue during recovery', claims Rowden. 'We spend whatever it takes during an emergency. If you're waiting patiently for someone to decide to release the funds, it's obviously not an emergency.'

When the dust has settled, literally, the loop from *doing* to *thinking* and *planning* is closed. Rowden observes that 'After each disaster, we are required to do an after-action report. Every once in a while something [in our plan] has to be changed.'

SUMMARY

To summarize, *thinking* about earthquake risk means understanding the possible damage and deciding what amount would be intolerable. *Planning* is the dual process of creating laws and a contingency plan that together can limit the damage to the stated appetite. Before an earthquake, *doing* is enforcing the law and rehearsing the plan; afterwards, it's search, rescue and recovery.

The way that Californians manage earthquake risk reflects three important facts about California. First, it is rich, with a per capita income of over $37,000 in 2005. Second, the history of California is one of taming a hostile environment. Third, the state bureaucracy is functional. Californians have the money, the mindset and the institutions to tackle even rare events like earthquakes.

Pakistan is in an earthquake zone. It would have been possible to calculate how much damage could be done to whom by earthquakes there. Given this damage, it would also have been possible to predict numbers and types of casualties, and to work backwards through the logistics that would be involved – opening roads, providing shelter, obtaining supplies and so on. The disorganization of the response suggests that this process simply did not take place. Whether from poverty, mindset or poor governance, the Pakistani authorities implicitly accepted a very high risk appetite and paid a high price. Since the earthquake, the Pakistani government has created two new agencies, the Federal Relief Commission and the Earthquake Reconstruction and Rehabilitation Agency. It remains to be seen to what extent they will manage damage prevention as well as disaster recovery.

Elsewhere, earthquakes seem to inspire fatalism. They seem to many to be the archetypical 'act of God'. Hiroaki Ubukawa works at Oyo-RMS, a Japanese firm that models natural disasters for insurance companies. He observes that '[many] people feel that natural hazards can't be helped. If it happens, it happens... you can't control it... people didn't think about quantifying risks. This approach is just taking root [in Japan].' This despite the fact that '10 per cent of all earthquakes on Earth are in the Japan region'. Perhaps, he speculates, this is because 'human beings are [innately] optimistic. After a tragedy we only remember for a short while. If you forget then you can survive.' Alternatively, it may just be that 'we cannot be on alert for ever. People have incorporated the risk into their daily life [and] they think it won't happen to them.' Either way, the earthquake risk management process in Japan is converging with the Californian process over time. For example, as in California, 'local authorities are responsible for emergency response. Someone in each district is designated the emergency response officer.'

APPLICATIONS TO BUSINESS

There are three lessons for risk managers in business from earthquake risk management. First, if your business is located in an earthquake zone, you can reuse the process described above. The first step is to obtain an earthquake shakemap to evaluate the frequency and severity of shocks at your location. An architectural assessment of your facilities will then tell you what damage your facilities will incur under different shocks. Comparing this damage estimate with your corporate risk appetite will then indicate how to plan for earthquake risk. The plan will consist of both required structural reinforcements and a contingency plan to ensure recovery afterwards.

Second, earthquakes show that having no explicit risk appetite doesn't mean you have no appetite for risk. It's just an implicit, decentralized, potentially incoherent appetite rather than an explicit, centralized, co-herent one. In Pakistan's case, the disorganized response implied a high risk appetite, probably higher than the government would have chosen had it gone through an explicit process – and certainly higher than the citizens of Pakistan would have chosen.

In business, the fact that you don't talk about an explicit risk appetite doesn't mean you're not taking risk. It just means that you have no benchmark, no way of knowing whether a given risk is large or small. For example, US investment banks have a sophisticated understanding of risk. They would certainly have been aware at some level that there was a conflict of interest between their duties to clients and their duties to investors in the way they lavished 'buy' recommendations on internet start-ups, such as Pets.com, whose initial public offerings (IPOs) they were underwriting. CBS's *60 Minutes* reported in 2001 that:

> Not even a company's imminent collapse could force analysts to say sell. Much of Pets.com's financing was raised by Merrill Lynch. Merrill made millions. Merrill's analyst Henry Blodgett made a buy recommendation

at $16. When it fell to $7, Blodgett said 'buy' again. Again a 'buy' at $2 and again at $1.69. When it hit $1.43 a share, Blodgett told investors to 'accumulate'. Pets.com was recently kicked off the stock exchange.

It appears that the investment banks never really considered the downside and compared it with their risk appetite elsewhere. They just implicitly thought 'We'll manage through it, how bad could it be?'

Quite bad, as it turns out. Merrill Lynch settled with New York Attorney General Elliot Spitzer. In addition to a $100 million fine and a public 'statement of contrition', the settlement separated research from investment banking and forced a re-evaluation of the strategic fit of advice and investment management under the same roof. In 2006, Merrill sold its investment management arm to BlackRock.

After the bankruptcies of Enron, Worldcom and others, in 2003 and 2004 Citigroup put aside nearly $7 billion to cover future litigation claims. If a trading business had held the possibility of a $7 billion loss, Citigroup would surely have closed it down. However in this case, it seems that although the firm recognized there was a risk, it hadn't lost any money yet, so it hadn't bothered to size it and compare it with the other risks run in the course of business.

At the other end of the spectrum, the lack of an explicit risk appetite means that you have no way to push back if you perceive that high risks are being taken, since 'high' is relative to what? It is better to be explicit and consistent about risk appetite, even if it can't be strictly quantified, since it ensures that there will be fewer nasty surprises.

Third, earthquakes are unexpected in the sense that you know they'll occur with a certain frequency and severity, but they'll hit without warning. There's no gradual build-up like a flood. In business, events also occur that you can't predict. In the abstract it is possible to say that bad outcomes may happen with a certain frequency and severity, but there is no advance warning, and the event is different each time.

Financial markets offer many examples. Market crashes (or 'corrections' if you prefer) occur suddenly, almost by definition out of the blue. If there were a pattern, banks would be able to recognize and plan for crashes – or even make money out of them. However, the trigger and the context are a bit different each time.

Like the ability to survive an earthquake, the ability to survive these events is determined by the resilience of the organization and the contingency management. Resilience means at one level having sufficient financial reserves to weather the losses. It also includes resilient IT systems, and operations that can continue to trade through difficult markets with abnormally high and volatile volumes. Alongside this, the human organization has to continue to function during the disruption. This will be a function of the quality of contingency planning and training, and the quantity of the resources available.

The resilience of Morgan Stanley during and after the attacks of 11 September 2001 was impressive. As with SEMS, if everyone knows what they are supposed to be doing and when, and they have the resources to be able to deliver, even a fragmented organization with disrupted information flows can continue to function. A centralized firm will be paralysed while decisions are made and communicated.

Without wanting to pun, the difference between the onset of a flood and the onset of an earthquake illustrates the effect of liquidity in markets. With liquidity, a market can absorb news of events steadily. Prices changes smoothly and continuously, and as in a flood, those who want to evacuate may do so. Without it, the market experiences a sudden disruption and prices may 'gap': that is, experience large jumps. There is no possibility of evacuation, only damage limitation. Illiquid markets are riskier than liquid markets for precisely this reason.

We have now finished our tour of risk management in extreme environments. Part II of the book summarizes the chapters and distils the seven laws of extreme risk management.

Part II

Themes

10

Managing risk in extreme environments

This chapter summarizes the key points of risk management in each of the extreme environments covered in the case studies in Chapters 1 to 9, and the *think–plan–do* framework from the Introduction. Chapter 11 then summarizes the transferable lessons for non-extreme environments, and the final chapter presents the 'seven laws of extreme risk management', which synthesize the main themes of the whole book.

THINK, PLAN, DO

Risk management everywhere follows the same process: first *think*, then *plan*, then *do*.

Thinking comes first. Before being able to manage risk, a risk manager must know how much risk is acceptable, and conversely at what stage to cut his or her losses. This appetite for risk is not self-evident. It is a philosophical choice, an issue of comfort with the frequency, severity and correlation of, and uncertainty around, potential events. Sometimes it is an individual choice, as in mountaineering; sometimes it is a group choice, as for example with cities in flood-prone areas.

Planning is next. There are two parts: a strategic plan that matches resources and risk appetite; and a tactical plan that assesses each individual risk faced and details the response to each one.

The first part is the big picture. If your risk appetite is very low but your environment is very risky, managing your risk is going to be both expensive and intrusive. It may be that simply leaving the environment is the best option.

If you decide to stay, the next stage is detailed planning. First, identify all the individual underlying risks, all the things that might go wrong. Then, assess and compare them to see which ones are the most likely and the most damaging. Finally, figure out what to do, who's going to do it, and how much that's going to cost.

Doing is a combination of activities. Before an event, *doing* means being prepared. This consists of recruiting, training and rehearsing response teams; acquiring and positioning the appropriate equipment, communications systems and budget; and ensuring that both the public and the response teams know what to do and what not to do. After an event, *doing* means keeping your wits about you while implementing the tactical plan, managing the inevitable unexpected events that crop up, and, to the extent possible, collecting data on the experience.

When the *doing* is over and the situation has returned to normal, risk managers must close the loop and return to *thinking*. Where performance was bad, the group must question whether the cause was local – training, procedures and equipment – or strategic – the situation was riskier than the organization wants to tolerate, or is able to afford. These conclusions feed into the next round of *thinking* and *planning*.

EPIDEMIC

In managing the risk of unknown infectious diseases, *doing*, not *thinking*, is the core of the process. *Doing* consists of five elements: characterize and understand the disease, creating treatment protocols and if possible a vaccine; contain the spread of the outbreak by isolating patients and protecting health care workers (HCWs); communicate the risks and required preventive behaviours to the public and HCWs; create surveillance and detection mechanisms to provide early warning of future outbreaks; and to the extent possible, influence the upstream ecosystem that supports the disease.

Thinking about the risk of unknown infectious diseases is a reactive, collective and implicit process. It is reactive, in that a society sets its risk appetite in response to recent outbreaks. The more recent and more severe the outbreak the lower the risk appetite (and the stronger the link from doing back to thinking). It is also collective and implicit, in that this appetite is expressed indirectly through tolerance of public health spending, rather than as an explicit statement of risk tolerance.

Planning around this risk appetite is then the process of matching the available resources to the highest priority actions required to manage the risk. The lower the risk appetite, the greater the spend, and thus the greater the opportunity to research the disease, communicate with the public, change upstream behaviours and implement early warning measures. Similarly, the lower the risk appetite, the greater the tolerance for restrictions on civil liberties that assist containment.

This approach implicitly assumes that the long-term risk level is stable. However, with our liberal use of biochemical 'cures', our increasing propensities to urbanize and to travel, and our intrusion into ecosystems hitherto undisturbed by humans, we have changed the world in which we live. The unintended consequence of these changes is that the risk of unknown infectious disease outbreaks may once more be increasing.

WILDFIRE

Our intervention in forest ecosystems has also increased the risks in the long term. Suppressing every fire seemed an obvious way to reduce fire risk. However, forests have evolved to tolerate and exploit fire; it is part of the ecosystem. Remove fire from the ecosystem and instability results. Suppressing all fires simply exchanges small, frequent fires now for infrequent, massive, out-of-control blazes later. Such fires torch the crowns of trees and kill them, destroying the forest. Different forests have evolved to exhibit different inherent fire loads. We can only influence this load at the margin. Fundamentally, you have to let the forest do the *thinking* for you.

Planning in wildfire risk management is the process of influencing this natural fire load to protect property and timber, conserve habitat, recreational space and watersheds, and, increasingly, limit carbon emissions. Trading off these different objectives yields a 'managed' risk tolerance that the various interested parties can live with and afford, and the risk manager can aim for – even if it too may not be sustainable in the long term.

Before the fire season, fire risk is managed towards this level through fire prevention activities and controlled burning. During the fire season, fire-fighting resources are arrayed pre-emptively against fire threats as they emerge. *Doing* is then devising a management plan for a specific fire and using these resources to fight them. Each year the loop from *doing* back to *thinking* and *planning* is closed as the weather patterns and operational experiences of the fire season are added to the historical record.

TERRORISM

Had the US and UK governments gone through a similar process and analysed historical experiences in counter-terrorism and invasion, they might have embarked on a different course in Iraq. As it is, they have transformed Iraq into the most extreme environment covered in this book, with scores dying every day from terrorism in various forms.

When *thinking* about risk, Western civilian risk managers in Iraq accept the possibility of deaths but aim for zero casualties. They manage this appetite by following two rules. First, when *planning*, if intelligence indicates that the threat level is over their risk appetite, they simply don't leave their base. Second, when *doing*, if they are attacked, they ensure that their staff are sufficiently skilled and trained in their chosen tactical response – defensive or aggressive, escape or counter-attack – that they execute it effectively. Risk managers in Iraq go through the *plan/do* cycle several times a day.

As a last resort they can call on the military. The military uses the same framework of intelligence-led deployment of highly skilled and trained personnel, undertaking offensive counter-terrorism operations as well. They have a higher risk appetite than civilian agencies. As a result most of the westerners who have died in Iraq were military. The fact that the military tolerate casualties does not mean that they do not think about risk. They are not suicidal. Rather, it simply means that they are risk-seeking. They want to take risk, but intelligently.

In general, investing in better intelligence, harder targets and expert human resources improves terrorism risk management. Military intervention far upstream to manage domestic terrorism risk, as the US government and its allies have done, is extraordinarily risky and prone to unexpected consequences.

The same keys apply in principle to *planning* and *doing* terrorism risk management in peacetime. Harden the obvious targets; if intelligence indicates an imminent attack, close the target down; if an attack occurs, ensure that your response and rescue teams execute the recovery plan quickly and effectively.

One important difference is that in Iraq there is clarity around the level of risk. Everyone is at risk, every day. This is not the case in a country at peace: there are many more targets than terrorists, and intelligence is more ambivalent. Consequently thinking about risk management in peacetime is more subjective, becoming a collective societal trade-off between the perceived threat and the inconvenience of government interventions and controls. As with epidemics, recent memory tends to dominate.

EXTREME HUMANITARIAN AID

At the heart of thinking about risk in extreme aid environments, such as conflict or near-conflict zones, is a similarly subjective assessment. The critical task is assessing the risk of deliberate harm to aid workers. This sets the boundary of aid organizations' risk tolerance.

Planning in these environments then has two main components: negotiating a non-intervention agreement with local armed parties; and setting up emergency evacuation plans in case they renege. *Doing* in this context means ensuring the physical health and safety of aid workers through a combination of secure facilities, security policies, and maintaining readiness for an evacuation.

In humanitarian demining operations, there are two additional aspects to *doing*. First is the rigorous application of standard operating procedures to the process of demining. The second involves reaching a conclusion about how 'safe' a 'clear' area is, and communicating the residual risk effectively to the local population.

Continuously updating and communicating security assessments closes the loop between *doing* and *thinking*. Ensuring that there is a constant reference back to the original risk appetite should ensure that it does not get reset at escalating levels. In other words, don't let the water heat up around you, and end up like the proverbial frog in boiling water that doesn't jump out as the temperature rises.

MOUNTAIN

Boiled frogs also feature in risk management in the mountains. The most important part of risk management here is *thinking* clearly so that you can say 'no' when circumstances change and the risks move beyond your risk appetite. Maintaining this perspective while *doing* is equally critical. If bad weather descends, or if you plan an expedition that needs five healthy people and two get sick, turn back. Don't stay out on the mountain as the risk increases, thereby risking becoming a boiled frog.

When *planning*, match your equipment, skills and physical abilities to the objective. Trade off weight and speed to your risk appetite: the greater your tolerance for risk, the less equipment you need to take and the quicker you can move. Train to the level of the technical and physical challenge you expect to encounter. Extensive planning and training help avoid panic, and allow individuals to respond to small failures before they compound into big ones.

Unlike most other environments, members of the public are primarily responsible for their own risk management in the mountains. This is because they want it that way. They want to be in the mountains, voluntarily exposing themselves to risk.

MELTDOWN

Nuclear power plants are unnatural. Their risks are mostly man-made. Risk management in this environment starts with *thinking* about an explicit expression of risk tolerance. In the United Kingdom the nuclear industry works off a tolerance of one chance in 10,000 per year of a fatality resulting from a given source. This risk tolerance is enforced across all components and processes, and fed into the planning process as a design requirement. Engineers design the plant and write the operational procedures, and emergency managers create disaster recovery plans, in such a way that this tolerance is expected to be met.

The plant design and procedures and the emergency plans are the context for *doing*. *Doing* means creating a working environment where safety is embedded in everyone's actions, all the time. This is difficult since systems that are designed to very high tolerances break down very rarely, and the apparent absence of risk can induce complacency, particularly in such a physically mundane environment. The foundations of such a safety culture are training, both for day-to-day management and for emergencies, and ongoing refinement of designs and procedures based on lessons learnt.

However, this is not the end of the process of risk management, because risk can be managed but not eliminated. The designers of the Chernobyl plant never foresaw that it would end up in the operational state it was brought into prior to the major accident that occurred; still less that many of the safety systems would be turned off when it did. This kind of 'latent' risk is almost impossible to foresee, even with the best design engineers and emergency planners. The best training in the world cannot create infallible operators.

Therefore the final key element of risk management in this environment is humility – the acceptance and communication of the limits of certainty. While it may be difficult to acknowledge and communicate openly about the risks of a catastrophe, it is imperative. Humility also makes denial less likely. If you believe that the impossible might happen, unexpected events won't panic you, and you won't freeze.

EXTRACTION

While typically more exposed than other environments to natural events such as storms as a result of their locations, oil platforms and coal mines are also, ultimately, man-made environments. The risk management process is similar to that in nuclear power plants. *Thinking* about risk in this environment means picking a risk appetite, then *planning* facilities, equipment and procedures so that they function to that tolerance.

The first part of *doing* is enforcing these standards through the safety culture, ideally by leading from the top. Such a safety culture seems to be the only defence against creeping complacency induced by the absence of events. This process is conspicuously absent in many facilities, especially in the developing world.

The second part is coping with the unexpected. No matter how good your design and procedures, eventually something unexpected will happen. The key is to adjust the recovery plan to the environment and execute it rigorously, without accepting more risk as the situation deteriorates and implicitly increasing risk appetite on the fly.

FLOOD

The most important part of flood risk management is also related to risk appetite. However, it is the reverse situation. Rather than implicitly increasing risk appetite as the risk level rises, the issue is failing to provide protection up to the risk appetite and then having to stand back and watch the levees breach. It is tempting to announce a conservative risk appetite, then cut corners when implementing the expensive measures necessary to resist all lesser events. The temptation exists because, by definition, a low risk appetite implies protection against all but the rarest events, so the odds of being found out are low.

Although flood protection and evacuation plans are rarely tested, it is essential to fund them properly – or simply tell the truth and say that the risk appetite is in fact higher than previously stated. Rather than assuming that it won't happens, or that even if it did, the authorities would take care of it, risk managers need to have a plan that will withstand extreme circumstances.

Floods are predictable in space, time and intensity. It is possible to estimate with reasonable confidence where, when and how severely floods will occur. Consequently you can subject *planning* to disciplined cost–benefit analysis. If the cost of the flood protection exceeds the cost of the property to be protected, then it's not worth it.

Floods only occur after it has started to rain. If emergency plans are credible, much of the *doing* can be focused on preventive evacuation as the rain falls, rather than search and rescue afterwards. Successful evacuation requires openness, credibility and a thick skin. If you choose a low risk tolerance, since forecasts are uncertain it is inevitable you will be wrong more often than right when you call for an evacuation. You will be cast as Cassandra. Keeping quiet, or worse still pretending everything is fine, then being hit 'unexpectedly' by a storm are alternatives, but they are not risk management.

EARTHQUAKE

A similar issue of honesty is central to earthquake risk management. *Thinking* about earthquake risk means understanding the possible damage and deciding what amount would be intolerable. Like floods, earthquakes do not occur everywhere, and it is possible to get a detailed risk assessment for any given location. Unlike floods, earthquakes strike without warning, but are over quickly.

If a community's earthquake risk appetite is unaffordable, risk managers must resist the temptation to keep quiet and pretend that it isn't. *Planning* is the dual process of creating laws and a contingency plan that together can limit the damage to the stated appetite. Before an earthquake, *doing* is enforcing the law and rehearsing the plan; afterwards, it's search, rescue and recovery.

The next chapter summarizes the implications for non-extreme environments of the findings about risk management in extreme ones.

11

So what?

This chapter summarizes and synthesises the more concrete implications for business of risk management in extreme environments from each of the case studies. There are two types of implication. One applies the lessons from extreme risk management to the overall process of risk management. The other looks at specific examples of transferable lessons from individual extreme environments to other contexts.

LESSONS FOR THE RISK MANAGEMENT PROCESS

The most obvious lesson is to apply the *think–plan–do* cycle to corporate risk management. In most cases risk managers are so busy with the *doing* that it is easy to lose touch with the other parts of the cycle. As in extreme environments, explicitly *thinking* about risk and discussing risk appetite is sometimes a bit abstract, but it is utterly necessary. From the starting point that risk appetite is not zero, all institutions should periodically formally reassess and restate their risk tolerance with reference to the sorts of transactions that they do and do not want to do, and the sorts of losses they can and cannot tolerate. This reassessment is usefully embedded in the institution's top-down strategic planning process, since the strategic plan should provide guidance about profitability and volatility targets on the one hand, and target products, regions and customer segments on the other. The process of setting a risk appetite converts these targets into an estimate of acceptable losses (or better still, volatility of profits).

A bottom-up internal benchmarking analysis should complement the top-down assessment. This benchmarking should compare the risk of individual transactions that have been approved and declined in different parts of the business. This analysis should reveal both overall trends in risk appetite and any inconsistency in its interpretation in different parts of the business. If there is no consistent view on risk appetite, it becomes impossible to manage the institution's overall risk level and to make sound judgements about risk and return. If there is a trend, or if there is evidence of inconsistency, the chief risk officer (CRO) needs to get involved and ensure that all parts of the risk organization understand and enforce to the overall risk appetite. If there are legitimate grounds for inconsistency, then the organization can restate its appetite. It is critical that this restatement is explicit. It is all too easy to allow inconsistent decision making to gradually inflate an organization's risk appetite, since inconsistencies usually tend towards higher risks and higher rewards.

FROM *RETHINKING* TO *REPLANNING*

It is also possible to lose sight of the *planning* dimension. If there are changes to risk appetite, risk managers need to embed them in new incentives, policies, limits and contingency plans.

In most extreme environments the downsides of poor planning are obvious, and there is no difference in incentives between risk takers and risk managers, if indeed they are not the same people. In more mundane environments, incentives are the elephant in the room in risk management.

In almost all institutions, incentive schemes reward the upside of risk taking without applying a corresponding penalty on the downside. Trader compensation is the best example. Traders buy and sell assets with the firm's money in the expectation of increases or decreases in asset prices. If they make a lot of money on these assets, they get a share of the profit, often a large amount. If they lose a lot of money, they get fired and they lose only their salary, usually a small fraction of their total compensation. They share the upside but not the downside of their risk taking.

Such asymmetric compensation schemes, lubricated with other people's money and operating in markets that often produce large gains and losses in very short periods, make it rational to take the largest positions possible, regardless of risk appetite. This is a natural source of risk appetite inflation, and can lead to institutions taking more risk than they want to. It also encourages fraud, for example by fudging mark-to-market values of positions, and arbitraging internal risk measurement systems by making risky trades that internal systems can't measure properly.

Risk managers need to lobby for compensation schemes that ensure those taking the risk feel some pain if things go badly. Such schemes include bonuses that depend on group as well as individual contribution, and deferred, illiquid or contingent compensation. They align an individual's incentives with those of the organization, encourage him or her to stick around for longer, and dampen the temptation to take excessive risk.

As a result of these difficulties in aligning incentives, and also strategic business decisions and simple uncertainty, risk managers articulate risk policies to constrain business practices. Policies describe the risk appetite in terms of what sort of business the institution does and does not want to do. Policies often collide with incentives, as deals surface that are outside policy but present a great upside to the surfacers and/or the institution.

As noted above, policies need to be refreshed in line with the thinking of the institution. Beyond that, exceptions to policy should be just that – exceptional. If the policies embed the risk appetite of the firm, then overriding them is another form of risk appetite dilution. Policy exceptions are the business equivalent of under-funding the levees but not communicating the implied change in risk appetite. They also accumulate independently in different business units, leading to barely visible inconsistency in risk appetite over time. Risk managers need to be open about the risk appetite implications of frequent policy exceptions, if only to ensure that the rules are relaxed evenly everywhere.

Risk limits come in two flavours: 'speed bumps' and 'hard limits'. Speed bump limits are set below the risk appetite. Their purpose is not to prohibit a deal, but rather to escalate discussion as risk levels increase. This ensures that risk taking in different parts of the business is consistent.

As in extreme environments, hard limits are set at the appetite for loss, and should not in general be overridden. Hard limits are what prevent you from becoming a boiled frog. Hard risk limits are cascaded from the top of the organization to each subordinate unit. Speed bump limits are then derived from these hard limits. If there are changes to risk appetite, these should cascade down the organization through changed limits.

MODELS

This cascading is not necessarily a simple process. Risk appetite, expressed as 'possible losses', is a statistical construct. To align incentives, policies and limits with the risk appetite, risk managers need to employ models. The literature on these models would fill a library. In this context this issue presents two key points, which apply in extreme and non-extreme environments alike.

The first point is to match the sophistication of the models to the sophistication of the problem to be solved. If you don't take exotic risks, you don't need exotic risk models. If the institution wants to increase market share in higher-margin, more exotic transactions, risk managers have to explain that the risk of exotic transactions costs more to evaluate. Exotic transactions are not higher margin for nothing, they are higher risk as well; there's no free lunch.

The second point, drawn directly from modelling natural hazards such as floods and fires, is to rely on real data as much as possible. Real data is always messy, sometimes hard to interpret, and usually boring and expensive to obtain. How much easier, more interesting and less expensive it is to build a model rather than grind out the data set. How tempting it is therefore to try to beat whatever limited data you have into the shape you want.

There are many tools on the data torturer's rack, from 'missing data algorithms' to various forms of 'bucketing' and smoothing, to powerful 'optimization' techniques with strong assumptions about the underlying form of the data, and extrapolation from where the data lies to where you want it to be. Afterwards, this 'data cleansing' and its embedded assumptions can be airbrushed away, since after all there is no data to prove or disprove them. Risk managers should resist this temptation. They must hold their nose, embrace the data with all its warts, and build the best historical data set they can.

In extreme cases, as for flood and fire modelling, this may take years. However, it is critical to the legitimacy of the risk management function. First, it is the best way to explain to non-technical audiences what a model does. Non-technical people reason backwards from their own experience, not forwards from a model specification. If their experience matches the model output, what the model does will make sense to them, and they may be able to work backwards into the technical side. At a minimum, if it makes sense to them, they will believe it – and, more importantly, they will believe you. If you can't get people to this point, they will not trust your advice.

In addition, the fact that the risk management area has gone through an exhaustive effort to compile a comprehensive and correct historical database, and to minimize the amount of torture inflicted upon it, is a credible signal that risk management is objectively interested in the truth. This claim is central to the legitimacy of the risk management function. Being open about the limitations of the data and the models makes risk managers more credible, not less, and opens the critical debate on what exactly we mean by risk anyway. Conversely, by relying on models and assumptions rather than engaging in the real world, risk managers reinforce the common perception that they are more interested in some sort of Platonic ideal world than what's going on around them.

This is not to say that risk managers should not use sophisticated models. Risk managers *should* use sophisticated models, if they are managing sophisticated product exposures and be open about the models' strengths and weaknesses. However, risk managers *should not* use modelling techniques to escape the inconveniences of real data, torture the data so that it tells them everything they want to know, or get so enamoured of their own creation that they retreat from the real world. Real data, however ugly, are real life, and there's only so much they can tell you.

CONTINGENCY PLANNING

Contingency planning in risk management usually focuses on business continuity, the logistical response to an interruption in normal activity. This is a valuable activity. Learning from extreme environments, alongside or as part of business continuity planning, risk managers should also develop contingency plans for extreme events: a market crash, terrorist attack, major customer bankruptcy, or fraud (or even a positive business event such as a takeover).

These plans need not be complicated, but they must be clear. They have to define the procedures, roles and responsibilities in extreme circumstances. Every risk manager should know what his or her role would be in a crisis situation, and what steps he or she would be expected to take, even if the CRO were en route to Shanghai and unavailable for comment, for example. In particular, risk managers should know the triage procedure: as the emergency level escalates, what is the order in which they can pare back their normal tasks?

The mere existence of clear contingency plans is insufficient, though. The plans need rehearsals. Risk managers should simulate emergencies periodically, beyond merely practising the fire drill. This way, risk managers will gain experience of operating under stress, thereby creating the 'breathing space' identified in the case studies. While there are few facilities that provide such simulations for financial services, other service organizations such as Reuters use simulations for exactly these purposes. They confine reporters to a simulated newsroom for a week. After three days of simulating coverage of a World Bank event by bombarding them with news releases and snaps, they feed reporters reports of a bomb threat, then of an explosion, then of an insurrection and so on. It's intense.

In addition to providing clarity and practice, senior risk managers also need to leave both surge capacity and flexibility in their organization to cope with unexpected events. Under constant pressure to cut costs against a background of increasing product and market sophistication and regulatory demands, many risk organizations are thinly staffed. Without some excess capacity, emergency response will be slower at exactly the time when speed is critical.

CROs can build surge capacity and flexibility into risk organizations without CEOs accusing them of empire-building, through a combination of staff selectivity and continuous improvement project work. Selectivity means choosing staff who are both able and self-confident enough make their own decisions in a crisis. In an emergency, the CRO needs staff whom he or she can trust to solve problems early and well, rather than delegating them upwards and waiting around for an answer as events compound. Equally, key staff need to know that they are trusted to solve those problems by themselves. Selective staffing also has the beneficial side-effect of improving the risk management area's overall performance and increasing its credibility with other business areas.

The CRO's problem is that such staff tend to be expensive and have short attention spans. Genuine continuous improvement projects can help to both justify and retain them. They allow able and self-confident people to solve difficult problems and have an impact on the organization. They can be oriented to cost reduction at least some of the time, thereby helping to placate the CEO. Happily they also are easily deferrable and can create surge capacity. The challenge for the CRO is to commit to continuous change rather than a quiet life.

That said, a commitment to continuous change has to be balanced against the risk of unexpected consequences. The bigger the change project, the further upstream it will aim to make changes. Risk managers should be cautious about 'silver bullet' solutions that appear to offer every hope of eliminating a problem, especially if the distance from cause to effect is large. The situation is always more complicated than they imagine.

Finally, risk managers will often be wrong. Organizations should accept that this is not the result of personal fallibility, but of the nature of risk itself. Risk managers will often have to bear the slings and arrows of outrageous fortune; their peers will often feel tempted to launch them. However, in the long run, both sides need to recognize that good risk managers are simply doing their job by pointing out the potential consequences of actions and transactions.

SPECIFIC LESSONS

Let's now move on to specific applications of extreme risk management techniques to non-extreme environments. The most obvious concerns disaster *planning*. Terrorism, earthquakes, floods and epidemics were four of the extreme environments analysed. Many operational risk managers face one or more of these threats. They can usefully copy the approach of the extreme risk managers profiled in these chapters (to the extent that they don't already). For example, those businesses in earthquake or flood zones should obtain 'shakemaps' and floodmaps respectively, evaluate the damage that occurs at the level of their chosen risk appetite, and develop contingency plans accordingly.

In our analysis of epidemic risk management, we encountered outbreak models that used the actual personal and work contacts between individuals to predict the spread of a disease. Both credit and market risk management could benefit from introducing such techniques as a complement to the current approach, where relationships between firms (correlations) are typically modelled indirectly. While data intensive, bolting together structural form credit risk models with real data on contagion channels between companies offers a more direct way of modelling portfolio risk than at present.

On the market risk side, regulators and institutions that handle large order flows will be able to surface links between apparently unrelated assets by working backwards to the portfolios that hold them. These links will show where stress in one asset class might induce stress in an unconnected asset class through shared holdings of portfolio managers: as one holding declines in value, they sell other, unrelated holdings. This is particularly relevant today, with the growth of asset management firms such as hedge funds that have few constraints on their investment strategy.

Because fires are part of a forest ecosystem, the immediate suppression of every forest fire weakens a forest in the long term. Similarly, 'fires' – economic problems – at individual companies are a natural part of an economy. Their immediate suppression by financial institutions weakens both the overall economy and the institution's portfolios in the long term. Institutions should avoid the temptation to suppress every fire, by for example restructuring credit to 'burning' customers or holding on to 'burning' trading positions. Recurrent fires may well indicate underlying problems that require a less expedient but more thorough solution.

The nuclear power industry attracts some of the best minds in physical science. The most successful of them are rewarded with praise and prestige. Financial services attract some of the best minds, period, in some cases from the nuclear industry. The most successful among them are rewarded with praise and money. Over time, the best minds may start to believe that their brilliance immunizes them from the unexpected. Over-confidence, even hubris, may set in.

However, the unexpected is inevitable. In the nuclear power industry this can cause thousands of deaths and catastrophic contamination. In finance, it may mean the end of an institution. Risk managers should learn from the history of the nuclear industry to guard against the emergence of hubris. One way to do this is to record and analyse near-misses as well as actual loss events. Typically, this preserves the sense that luck as well as skill plays a role in loss avoidance. Another is to encourage staff movement within the risk area, so that periodically risk managers are forced out of their comfort zone.

Earthquakes occur with a known frequency and severity. However, there is no warning, so there is no opportunity for evasive action. The only option is to build a resilient recovery organization, which can start up at short notice under great stress. In business too, events occur that you can't predict. In abstract it is possible to say that bad outcomes may happen with a certain frequency and severity at certain locations, but there is no advance warning of a specific instance. Moreover, unlike an earthquake, the event is different each time. Financial markets offer many examples of these unexpected events, such as market 'crashes'. These are always unexpected, in that if market participants believed a crash was on the way, they would have sold out already.

Like the ability to survive an earthquake, the ability to survive these events is determined by the resilience of the organization. Risk managers should aim to build resilient organizations that have sufficient financial and human resources that they can cope with unexpected, sudden events. This is related to the concept of contingency planning, but is more specific in that it requires that an organization cope with crises without warning.

Mountaineers are primarily responsible for their own risk management. However, many mountaineers are only in the mountains for short periods of time. This means that they are more likely to go ahead with an expedition even if the risks are beyond their risk appetite. After all, they only get a couple of weeks a year, and how bad could it get? This is analogous to the 'sunk cost fallacy' in investment decisions. Sunk cost is the amount of money you have already spent on a project. If something happens well into a project that changes the risk profile, there's a temptation to continue regardless rather than 'waste' all the money already spent. After all, how bad could it get?

If conditions have changed so much that a project is no longer worthwhile looking forward, risk managers should argue for the project's termination, irrespective of how much money has already been sunk into it. The money spent is irrecoverable, so it shouldn't have any bearing on your decisions going forward.

Finally, in extreme aid situations, aid agencies negotiate a non-intervention guarantee from local armed powers. This has no force in law, but if the right social and personal conditions are in place, it can work to protect aid workers. Similarly business transactions are also sometimes undertaken on the basis of a 'soft' guarantee, one that has weight personally but not legally. There are two lessons that transfer. One is that even as an institution enters into a transaction, it should be making an evacuation plan just in case. The other is that if it ever appears that the guarantee has expired, or no longer carries any weight, don't wait around to find out whether this is really the case. Leave immediately. Otherwise you risk observing the worst-case scenario up close and personal.

There are seven key themes that cut across all the extreme environments – indeed all environments. These seven themes are elaborated in the next chapter.

12

The seven laws of extreme risk management

One purpose of this book is to illustrate core risk management concepts using examples drawn from extreme environments. This concluding chapter distils seven risk management themes from the preceding chapters.

1 DEATH FOCUSES THE MIND

In life and death environments it is easy to end up dead. As a result, those who survive long term in extreme environments tend to be excellent risk managers – even if they tend to have trouble understanding what exactly is meant by 'risk management'. If your own life is at stake, you don't need procedures, manuals, restricted stock allocations or performance targets to pay attention to risk and manage it. You just get on with it because otherwise you'll die.

One consequence of this is that risk managers in extreme environments, such as mountain rescue or counter-terrorism, are rigorous about learning from their experiences. In almost all cases, there is a requirement to feed back into the thinking process not just experiences of actual events but also 'near-misses'. They are as interested in what almost happened and what might have happened as what actually happened, as this enables them to anticipate risks as they emerge rather than reacting to them afterwards.

The best risk management systems work by reproducing this alignment of interests, where the individual shares both some of the risk and some of the reward. The worst risk management systems create 'moral hazard' where individuals get the reward but not the risk, and hence have an incentive to take as much risk as they can get away with.

Lesson: record and analyse near-misses; align the interests of the risk managers and the risk takers by sharing both the upside and the downside of the business.

2   HONESTY MATTERS

Thinking about risk and defining a risk appetite can seem abstract in most circumstances. In extreme environments they are anything but. In such environments, not being honest with yourself or others about risk appetite can make the difference between life and death.

One way in which honesty matters is when a risk manager develops plans around a given risk appetite, then concludes that the costs are too high. For example, a city might want protection against a 1 in 100 year storm, but the costs of that level of flood control would be beyond the city's means.

There is a choice at this point. The risk manager can reason that 100 years is a long time, and the storm will probably not hit while he or she is still in the job. Or, the risk manager can decide to tell the city the bad news: that either they need to choose a more affordable risk appetite, or they need to find more money from somewhere.

Silence is tempting in a world where few people remain in jobs more than a couple of years, and being honest would be very uncomfortable. Many choose the silence. They do not challenge the publicly stated risk appetite even as they can't fund the projects, person power and equipment necessary to meet it. The risk appetite of the city slips down from 1 in 100 years. Eventually, a storm of less than a 1 in 100 year severity hits and causes catastrophic damage, and the slippage is revealed. Dishonesty about risk appetite will inevitably be exposed. In an extreme environment this will result in people dying.

The second type of dishonesty is more personal. For example, aid workers destined for a post-conflict situation or climbers attempting a summit may agree on a low risk appetite before going. Once underway, however, circumstances are usually so different that it is hard to keep this original risk appetite in mind. In addition, the risk level usually increases slowly, like a rising tide. In this situation it is possible to rationalize each individual event and ignore the overall pattern. As the risk level increases, individuals' risk appetites stretch to accommodate the increase without acknowledgement. Then something truly awful happens and the true level of risk is undeniable. By then, it may be too late to reduce risk back to the appetite. Once again, dishonesty ends up costing lives, even if in this case it is likely to be the individual's own life rather than those entrusted to his or her care.

Lesson: if you can't afford your risk appetite, speak up. Preserve your original risk appetite, don't stretch it thoughtlessly over increasing risk.

3   REALITY BEATS SIMULATION

Highly trained, highly motivated staff are expensive. So are the tools of their trade, from fire engines to helicopters to computerized operations centres. Since extreme events are rare, it is difficult to gauge the resources required at a given risk appetite. Too few, and they will be overwhelmed; too many and they will get bored and rusty.

Simulation models can breed extreme events to study. These models are used in two very valuable ways. First, as part of the ongoing planning process they are used to assess damage under different extreme scenarios. For example, the UK Environment Agency simulates extreme weather and tides in London to see the depth to which each part of the city would be underwater in each scenario. The depth information shows how many people would have to be evacuated, and what emergency response resources would be unavailable (for example, which water treatment plants and power stations would be flooded). This in turn indicates the emergency response resource requirements. The models also allow the inclusion and assessment of hypothetical flood defences.

Second, simulations are used to plan the response to emerging threats in real time. For example, while a storm is still offshore in the Gulf of Mexico, simulation models can predict its path and likely impact in New Orleans or Houston. With each hour that passes, the results become more accurate. These results can play an important role in persuading people in the path of the storm to evacuate before it's too late.

The decreasing cost of computing power means that these models are increasingly powerful, integrating more ever data across ever-larger areas in ever more detail. The line between reality and model blurs. Faced with such sophistication, it is tempting to substitute the model for reality. This is a mistake. Models are only models, reality simplified so that our poor inadequate minds can grasp a slice of it. Reality is always more complex than we can reproduce in a model.

While simulation directs powerful mathematical techniques at large data sets to produce apparently precise results, there are always many assumptions and much subjectivity buried in the model. This is especially true in the treatment of human behaviour. For example, if a hospital-based epidemic such as SARS broke out, at what point would people decide that going to hospital was more dangerous that staying at home? Would they then try to get away by travelling, or shut themselves up at home? No one knows. While there are some historical precedents, the same circumstances rarely recur, and in any case human behaviour is not static, it evolves. Models simulate reality, but they are not real.

One way to avoid model enslavement is to research history thoroughly. A database of every historical incident is a very powerful tool for understanding risk and for communicating it. For example, both Nick Collins, London Fire Brigade's head of strategic risk management, and Marc Castellnou, head of fire management strategy at the Catalan Forest Fire Service, log real data on fires rather than relying purely on simulation.

In addition to simulation models on computers, it is possible to build physical simulators to mimic the experience of certain extreme events. Flight simulators are the gold standard for physical simulators. The size of small trucks, they provide pilots with an experience that is extremely close to that of flying a real plane. Although not quite as realistic, in that they lack the physical sensations provided by flight simulators, there are simulators for most control rooms, such as oil rigs and nuclear power plants. Simulator sessions are a requirement for many positions, such as pilots or offshore installation managers. They too are still not quite the same as real experience. However, by simulating emergencies, the simulators allow staff to gain experience of extreme events without the life and death baggage, and risk managers to test whether their plans work in practice.

Lesson: models are valuable tools, but they're only models. Don't be blinded by the brilliance of the modellers. Use real data if possible, and physical simulation if available.

4   STANDARDS DRIVE SUCCESS

Even when your own life is at stake, it is possible to freeze in the face of danger. Risk managers in extreme environments counter this tendency by imposing rigorous standards for personnel selection and training, and for operating procedures. They select people who are physically and mentally robust – 'Personal characteristics and qualities than can't be taught, such as determination, robustness, and integrity' in the words of a serving UK Special Forces lieutenant colonel. They then train them under harsh conditions. The Glencoe mountain rescue teams practise 'climbing steep mountains in bad weather'.

They ensure that standard operating procedures, especially communications protocols, are well defined, well understood and well rehearsed. Thus the response to a major incident of any type, anywhere in California, will follow the same pattern, as defined by the Standard Emergency Management System (SEMS). Each participant knows the system and their role in it, and will have rehearsed it. And they ensure that their staff know that they are in tactical control of the situation, with both managerial latitude and some spare capacity to respond to changing conditions if they see fit. Thus Médecins sans Frontières (MSF) delegates full control of local security to the local logistics and security manager. If he or she decides the risk level has crossed the threshold and it's time to leave, there will be no retrospective judgement with the benefit of hindsight from the centre.

The net effect is to create a team of highly capable individuals who can execute their part of the risk management plan independently. This means that if (when) communication breaks down during an emergency, they all know what they're supposed to be doing and get on with it, in parallel. As communication is re-established, the risk management organization rebuilds itself from the bottom up even as it executes the original risk management plan. In addition, the empowerment of highly capable individuals means that they won't freeze, pass the buck and wait for orders in the face of unexpected events. They will intervene and stop events compounding one on top of another. This intervention can make the difference between an accident and a catastrophe.

Lesson: select robust people who can cope with extreme events. Train them so that they are comfortable in extreme situations. Give them some latitude and spare capacity, standardize operational procedures and rehearse them intensively.

5   BEWARE UNINTENDED CONSEQUENCES

It seemed like a good idea at the time. When the US Forest Service stated its '10 by 10' rule – all fires over ten acres under control by 10.00am the next day – it undoubtedly appeared to be a good solution to the problem of forest fires. Why wait for a fire to approach developed areas and suffer the damage? Get there fast, put it out fast. What could be simpler?

However, the forests needed fire to remain in equilibrium. The long-term effect of the policy was the accumulation of fuel in denser forests. Fire patterns became unstable: the fires became bigger and more destructive.

Fire fighters encountered more fires that they couldn't control. The Forest Service attacked fires more aggressively, with more personnel and more machines. The fires got still bigger and yet more destructive. After the most intense fires, the forest simply died.

Eventually, a more holistic view prevailed. Forests in dry environments have evolved to survive and exploit fires. Fire plays an important role in healthy forests by burning back saplings and preventing the accumulation of brush on the forest floor. Fire managers the world over are now integrating this idea into their risk management strategies.

These situations are surprisingly common. What seems a reasonable idea may turn out to make things worse. It appears that the invasion of Iraq may increase the frequency of terrorist attacks on Americans. The Mississippi Gulf Outlet, a heavily subsidized shipping channel that promised prosperity to New Orleans, acted as a funnel that amplified the Katrina storm surge and contributed directly to the collapse of the levees and the destruction of the city. The widespread availability of antibiotics brings forward the day when none of them will work.

The world is a complex and uncertain place. Any single risk management tactic that appears to offer a short cut may well have a hidden downside. This is especially so when the distance between cause and effect is large. Risk managers should be cautious about such tactics, since the cure can sometimes be worse than the disease.

Lesson: it's always more complicated than you think. Beware simple solutions, especially if the distance between cause and effect is large.

6   STUFF HAPPENS

Bad things happen often in extreme environments. Dozens of people a day are dying violent deaths in Iraq. Risk is unavoidable and risk management is clearly necessary.

In less extreme environments bad things happen rarely. For example, a passenger airliner had not been hijacked in the United States for almost 30 years prior to 11 September 2001. It was possible to think that the risk had gone away, that risk management was unnecessary, or that effective risk management had stopped hijacks from happening. As the events of that day demonstrated, in this case it hadn't, it wasn't and it didn't.

Even in everyday environments, risk is ever-present. There is no certainty. Risk management supplies a framework to think rationally about this fact of life. Good risk management helps reduce the severity, and sometimes the frequency, of bad things. It does not mean risk elimination and never could.

Lesson: don't be surprised when bad things to happen, however good you think your risk management may be.

7 RISK MANAGERS NEED A LOUD VOICE AND A THICK SKIN

In Greek legend, Cassandra, the daughter of the king of Troy, is doomed to prophesy the truth but not be believed. Among her successful but unheeded predictions was that the Trojan horse was not a gift but full of Greek soldiers intent on raping and pillaging.

Risk managers can relate. The problem is that risk is uncertain, so predictions about risk are doubly uncertain. The rarer the event, the more uncertain the prediction. Risk managers will often be wrong. This structural inaccuracy means that risk managers have to balance communication with credibility. If they communicate too frequently, people will simply tune out their warnings. If they communicate too infrequently, there will be little awareness or understanding of the risk. Most risk managers err on the side of frequency, and, like Walter 'Doctor Doom' Maestri in New Orleans, they have to grow a thick skin to cope with the sarcasm they meet after a few unfulfilled predictions.

There are a couple of best practices. Communication should be part of planning. The plan should cover the key messages, their delivery and timing. While there is a desire to reassure, information should dominate. For example, by combining the output of flood simulation models with mapping software on a website, it is possible to allow individuals to see a micro-forecast for the neighbourhood or even their home. Letting the public access the specific model results directly, rather than just listen to generic pronouncements, enhances credibility.

The other best practice is simply to make sure that there is a plan for dealing with incoming calls after an emergency. There's nothing quite like a perpetual busy signal to anger anxious relatives.

Lesson: make the tough calls; communicate often and through as many media as you can; don't take the criticism personally.

That seems an appropriate note to end on. I hope you have enjoyed this book. If you have any questions or comments, please drop me a line at duncan@lifeanddeathrisk.com.

'Best of' resources

This is not an exhaustive list of references. It is designed to guide you to those secondary sources I found especially useful, skipping the merely interesting and/or informative.

RISK MANAGEMENT

Bernstein, Peter (1998) *Against the Odds: The remarkable story of risk*, Wiley, Chichester

Bernstein, Peter (2005) *Capital Ideas: The improbable origins of modern Wall Street*, Wiley, Chichester

Marrison, Christopher (2002) *The Fundamentals of Risk Management*, McGraw-Hill Education, Maidenhead, Berks

Taleb, Naseem Nicholas (2007) *Fooled by Randomness: The hidden role of chance in life and the markets*, Penguin, London

EPIDEMIC

HK Government on SARS: http://www.sars-expertcom.gov.hk/textonly/english/reports/reports.html

WHO: http://www.who.int/en/

NHS: http://www.dh.gov.uk/PolicyAndGuidance/EmergencyPlanning/fs/en

US CDC: http://www.cdc.gov/

Ontario: http://www.health.gov.on.ca/index.html

Health Canada: http://www.hc-sc.gc.ca/dc-ma/index_e.html

Abraham, Thomas (2005) *Twenty-first Century Plague: The story of SARS,* Johns Hopkins University Press, Baltimore, MD

Centers for Disease Control and Prevention (CDC) (1998) *Preventing Emerging Infectious Diseases: A strategy for the 21st century overview of the updated CDC Plan,* CDC, Atlanta, Ga [online] http://www.cdc.gov/mmwr/preview/mmwrhtml/00054779.htm (accessed 1 June 2007)

WILDFIRE

California Office of Emergency Services: http://www.oes.ca.gov/Operational/OESHome.nsf/1?OpenForm

California Forest Service: http://www.fire.ca.gov/php/

Natural Resources Canada: http://www.nofc.forestry.ca/fire/index_e.php

New South Wales Forests: http://www.dpi.nsw.gov.au/forests

Pyne, Stephen J (2002) *Year of the Fires: The story of the great fires of 1910,* Penguin, London

TERRORISM

LFB: http://www.london-fire.gov.uk/

London Resilience: http://www.londonprepared.gov.uk/

UK Government: http://www.ukresilience.info/terrorism.htm

Department of Homeland Security: http://www.dhs.gov/index.shtm

National Counterterrorism Centre: http://www.nctc.gov/

White House: http://www.whitehouse.gov/nsc/nsct/2006/

The DVD of *Black Hawk Down* has a fascinating special feature in which the four technical advisors, three of whom fought in Mogadishu, give minute-by-minute commentary on the movie.

For more information on Blackwater, the *Virginian-Pilot* published an excellent series of in-depth articles in July 2006.

Singer, P W (2004) *Corporate Warriors: The rise of the privatized military industry,* Cornell Studies in Security Affairs, Cornell University Press, Ithaca, NY

Woo, Gordon (2007) Terrorism risk, in *Wiley Handbook of Science and Technology for Homeland Security,* Wiley, New York

EXTREME AID

MSF: http://www.msf.org/
STC: http://www.savethechildren.org.uk/scuk/jsp/index.jsp
NPA: http://apu.idium.no/folkehjelp.no/
UN: http://www.mineaction.org/
IMAS: http://www.mineactionstandards.org/imas.htm
Geneva International Centre for Humanitarian Demining (2004) *A Guide to International Mine Action Standards*, Geneva
Stoddard, Abby and Harmer, Adele (2005) *Room to Manoeuvre: Challenges of linking humanitarian action and post-conflict recovery in the new global security environment*, Human Development Report, UN Development Programme, New York

MOUNTAINS

PGHM: http://www.pghm-chamonix.com/
Glencoe Rescue: http://www.glencoe-mountain-rescue.com/index.htm
Mountain Tracks Guiding: http://www.mountaintracks.co.uk/
Extreme Everest Project: http://www.xtreme-everest.co.uk/
Krakauer, John (1998) *Into Thin Air: A personal account of the Everest disaster*, Pan, London
Simpson, Joe (1998) *Touching the Void*, Vintage, London

MELTDOWN

IAEA: http://www.iaea.org/
UKAEA: http://www.ukaea.org.uk/
Chernobyl: http://www.chernobyl.info/index.php
British Energy: http://www.british-energy.com/
Bodansky, David (2004), *Nuclear Energy: Principles, practices, and prospects*, 2nd edn, Springer-Verlag, New York
Perrow, Charles (1999) *Normal Accidents: Living with high-risk technologies*, Princeton University Press, Princeton, NJ

EXTRACTION

William Fisher's letter was sourced from The National Library of
Wales.
Conoco: http://www.conocophillips.com/index.htm
Anglo American: http://www.angloamerican.co.uk/
Roc Oil: http://www.rocoil.com.au/
Piper Alpha: http://www.oilandgas.org.uk/issues/health/faq.htm
Cullen, W Douglas (Lord) (1990) *The Public Inquiry into the Piper Alpha
Disaster*, The Stationery Office, London

FLOODING

New Orleans Times-Picayune: http://www.nola.com/
LSU Hurricane Centre: http://hurricane.lsu.edu/
UK Environment Agency: http://www.environment-agency.gov.uk/
subjects/flood/
National Oceanic and Atmospheric Administration: http://www.nws.
noaa.gov/

EARTHQUAKES

USGS: http://www.usgs.gov/
CGS: http://www.quakc.ca.gov/
California OES: http://www.oes.ca.gov/Operational/OESHome.nsf/1?
OpenForm
Charles B Sedgwick's account is from *Some Personal Observations on
the Fall of SF*, available online from the Virtual Museum of the City of
San Francisco: http:www.sfmuseum.org/1906.2/ew20.html.

OTHER

RMS: http://www.rms.com/
Junger, Sebastian (2007) *The Perfect Storm: A true story of men against
the sea*, rev edn, Harper Perennial, London
Kahneman, Daniel, Slovic, Paul and Tversky, Amos (eds) (1982) *Judge-
ment under Uncertainty: Heuristics and biases*, Cambridge University
Press, Cambridge, UK

Index